THE HEART OF A FATHER

malachi**dads**
LIFELINE GLOBAL MINISTRIES™

THE HEART OF A FATHER

LIFELINE
GLOBAL™

lifelineglobal.org

© 2020

3 4 5 17 16 15

FOREWORD

The Heart of a Father is a core Bible study of the Malachi Dads curriculum from Lifeline Global Ministries (formerly known as Awana Lifeline). For years this book has touched the lives of thousands of men and fathers around the world and has been taught mostly in jails and prisons but also in churches, homes, Dream Centers, to broken families and those dealing with an addiction.

Inmates around the world have been transformed by God's Word and His Holy Spirit. *The Heart of a Father* is a Christ-honoring Bible study that focuses on three areas:

1. How to be a godly man.
2. How to be a godley husband.
3. How to be a godly father.

God is using this tool to bring men to salvation in Christ by the thousands in 13 languages and 16 countries (as of this writing).

Our prayer for *The Heart of a Father* is that God would use it to bring hope to men (inmates) and that families would be reconciled to Christ and one another.

Chris Vance and Rod Martin are the authors of the original material. We are grateful for their faithful God-honoring work, using God's Word to bring the gospel of Christ to inmates.

John Reed and Jeffrey Steele have edited several lessons and have taught these lessons at LA County jails to thousands of men, faithfully seeing men come to faith in Christ. We honor their service and work with Lifeline Global Ministries.

"Only God."

Dr. Mike Broyles
Executive Director of Lifeline Ministries

TABLE OF CONTENTS

MALACHI DADS KEY VERSE

*And he will turn the hearts of fathers
to their children and the hearts of
children to their fathers....*

Malachi 4:6

FACILITATOR NOTES

LARGE GROUP PLAN

Begin the large group time with an opening prayer. Introduce the facilitators. Use first names only and remind participants that each facilitator is there to help them know God and learn how to live a life that honors God.

INTRODUCE THE PROGRAM AND GOALS

Begin the first lesson by briefly introducing the Malachi Dads program and goals. Use the following outline as a guide:

TIME	The group will meet for two hours each week over the next 12 weeks.
PURPOSE	Our goal is to provide an overview of what the Bible says about creation, God, men, salvation, marriage, and being a father.
FORMAT	We will start each meeting as one large group to introduce and teach the main topic, which will be different each lesson. Then we will break into small groups in order to accomplish the following: • Discuss the topic in more detail. • Consider choices and consequences. • Review homework. • Pray.

SMALL GROUP DISCUSSION RULES

- *One person talks at a time.*

- *No disrespectful comments. Only use positive, respectful language.*

- *Talk about yourself, not others.*

- *Make sure everyone gets a chance to talk.*

- *Stay focused.*

- *What people say in the group should stay in the group.*

KEY BELIEFS

These are important truths that our group believes:

- *God is real, and He is in charge of all things.*

- *God's Word is true. God gave us the Bible for our benefit and guidance. It is the owner's manual for human beings.*

- *The Bible is all we need to understand our world, and to live in a way that pleases God. Following the Bible allows us to help our families, neighbors, and country.*

KEY THEME

Our key theme for the entire study is "Two Paths."

- *Every day we must choose between two paths. We will either obey God or disobey God. We will choose to honor God or honor ourselves.*

- *There are consequences to each path.*

- *Each week in our small groups we will talk about the different choices we're facing, and which path those choices will take us on.*

KEY VERSE

Our key verse for the entire study is Malachi 4:6.

> *And he will turn the hearts of fathers to their children and the hearts of children to their fathers.*

THE MALACHI DADS PLEDGE

As a Malachi Dad, I solemnly pledge to glorify God and build His Kingdom by prioritizing the raising of godly children, first in my family, then in the influencing of other men to do the same in theirs. I firmly believe that my transformed life in Christ—my life of integrity, pursuit of this vision, and the pursuit of godly character—will allow me to impact my children, family, and others towards this end.

I will practice a life of daily discipline and dependence on God through prayer and the study of God's Word for the wisdom in how to nurture my children in the admonition of the Lord. I will pursue this endeavor for a lifetime whether my children are in my home or not.

Finally, I believe that my end goal is not only for my children to walk in the Lord but this God-given vision would impact multiple generations to come, so help me God.

Our goal throughout this study is to equip men to live out this pledge in their families and communities. It will come up in lessons 6, 8, 11, and 12.

LESSON 1 **MEMORY VERSE**

In the beginning, God created the heavens and the earth.

Genesis 1:1

Lesson 1: **Creation**

FACILITATOR NOTES

KEY TOPICS

- The Bible is our reliable guide for life, and is our only source for truth. It is the owner's manual for human beings.

- God is the Creator and Ruler of all things.

- People are God's creations who are made in His image and made to worship Him.

LARGE GROUP NOTES

Discuss the two major topics from Lesson 1: God and People. Use the bolded questions to help your group members get involved in the lesson and apply what they learn to their own lives.

Ask for volunteers to read any Bible verses out loud. (Or read them out loud yourself if that works best.)

The key point for the large group time to make is that God is the creator. He has made human beings, both males and females, unique and special. They are the only thing in all creation that is most like Him...bearing His image. This means we are personal beings like God so we can have a relationship with Him. We have a mind, will, and emotions like Him, and we are created to worship Him.

Be sure to focus on what it means to be an image bearer of God.

SMALL GROUP NOTES

Divide the large group into smaller groups of four to six people *(depending on the number of facilitators available). Using the bolded questions discuss the main topics of this week's lesson.*

A significant point to make clear in the small group time is that God as the Creator of all things has the right to design and make all the rules. He made everything, and everything has a function and a purpose for how it is designed to work.

Use the example of a manufacturer that has designed a product then provides a manual to the customer for how that item is to be used. If the product is not used correctly it can break. Sin is when we choose to go against God's intended purpose for us (we will talk more about sin in the next chapter).

Close the small-group discussion with a time of prayer.

Lesson 1

CREATION

LARGE GROUP SESSION

TOPIC 1: GOD

God is the Creator of all things.

> *In the beginning, God created the heavens and the earth. The earth was without form and void, and darkness was over the face of the deep. And the Spirit of God was hovering over the face of the waters.* —**Genesis 1:1-2**

What's something you created that you're proud of?

The book of Genesis is the first book in the Bible, and it sets the stage for everything that follows in God's Word. Genesis describes the creation of everything—time, the universe, people, marriage, and so on. All of these things were created by God in the beginning.

Because God is the Creator of everything in the universe, He is also the Ruler of everything He created.

> *The LORD has established his throne in the heavens, and his kingdom rules over all.* —**Psalm 103:19**

What was your favorite sport or game to play when you were a kid? Why?

Why was it important to know the rules for that sport or game in order to succeed?

God sets the rules for how the world should work and what we are supposed to do as part of His creation. That means we need to understand the rules so that we can succeed in life—just like we would need to know the rules to succeed in any game or sport. That's why we have the Bible.

TOPIC 2: PEOPLE

Human beings were created by God.

> Then God said, "Let us make man in our image, after our likeness. And let them have dominion over the fish of the sea and over the birds of the heavens and over the livestock and over all the earth and over every creeping thing that creeps on the earth." So God created man in his own image, in the image of God he created him; male and female he created them. —**Genesis 1:26-27**

Why is it important for us to understand that God is our Creator?

What does it mean to be created in the image of God?

To be created in the image of God means we share some characteristics with Him. God is personal; we are personal. God has a mind, will, and emotions; so do we. We are religious beings, created to have a relationship with Him.

Not only were human beings created in the image of God, we were also created with a specific purpose—to worship God and bring Him glory. Look at the first lines of the Westminster Catechism:

Question: What is the chief end of man?

Answer: Man's chief end is to glorify God, and to enjoy Him forever.

What does it mean to be a religious person?

How would you describe what it means to worship something or someone?

Webster's Dictionary defines *worship* as: "showing devotion, reverence, love, veneration, admiration to someone or something." All people were created with a desire to worship God, which means even people who don't believe in God always end up worshiping something else.

SMALL GROUP SESSION

DISCUSSING GOD

What have you learned about God during this lesson?

Do you have any questions about what we've covered so far?

> *Then the LORD God formed the man of dust from the ground and breathed into his nostrils the breath of life, and the man became a living creature.* —**Genesis 2:7**

> *By faith we understand that the universe was created by the word of God, so that what is seen was not made out of things that are visible.* —**Hebrews 11:3**

What do you find interesting about the verses we just read? What picture does the Genesis verse bring to mind?

If you believe that God created everyone, how should that impact the way you treat other people?

How should that impact the way you think about yourself?

God is the Creator of all things, which means He is also the Ruler of all things—including all people.

> Yours, O LORD, is the greatness and the power
> and the glory and the victory and the majesty,
> for all that is in the heavens and in the earth is
> yours. Yours is the kingdom, O LORD, and you are
> exalted as head above all. —1 Chronicles 29:11

Who is the main person in charge of these prison facilities?

What motivates you to obey that person? Why?

How is God similar to the person we just described? How is He different?

DISCUSSING PEOPLE

What have you learned about people during this lesson?

Do you have any questions about what we've covered so far?

> Hear, O Israel: The LORD our God, the LORD is
> one. You shall love the LORD your God with all
> your heart and with all your soul and with all your
> might. —Deuteronomy 6:4-5

When have you tried to worship something or someone instead of God? How did it go?

What does it mean to worship God?

> *But now, O LORD, you are our Father; we are the clay, and you are our potter; we are all the work of your hand.* —**Isaiah 64:8**

What do you like best about the verses we just read? Why?

In what ways would you like your relationship with God to grow during this study? What will you need to do to help that happen?

Lesson 1
HOMEWORK

Complete the following assignments before the group gathers for Lesson 2.

Read Psalm 1:1-6 and answer the following questions:

1. What are the two choices (two paths) described in this psalm?

2. What are the consequences of following each choice?

Read Proverbs 1:1-33 and answer the following questions:

1. What is wisdom?

2. What are some benefits of seeking wisdom?

3. How do we gain wisdom?

4. What are the consequences of ignoring wisdom?

Answer these questions about your life:

1. What is your main goal in life?

2. What makes you happier than anything else?

3. Who are the most important people in your life?

4. Who are the people you most want to impress?

5. Who or what have you been worshiping recently?

6. How will you intentionally worship God this week?

Review this week's memory verse:

> *In the beginning, God created the heavens and the earth.* —**Genesis 1:1**

LESSON 2 **MEMORY VERSE**

*For all have sinned and fall short
of the glory of God.*

Romans 3:23

Lesson 2 : **Sin**

FACILITATOR NOTES

KEY TOPICS

- *Definition for sin.*
- *Cause and consequences of our sin.*
- *Identifying Satan's strategy for attacking our weakness so that we will be ready when the attack comes.*

LARGE GROUP NOTES

Begin with an opening prayer.

Remind group members of the Malachi Dads program goals, discussion rules, and key beliefs, key theme, and key verse from pages 12-13.

Use the questions on pages 29-32 to address the topic of sin according to God's Word. These questions will help your group members get involved in the lesson and apply what they learn to their own lives.

Be sure to highlight that God made all of creation and that creation was good, perfect, and complete. This is a brief review from lesson 1.

The goal Satan had for tempting Adam and Eve was to challenge God's authority. In a way, what Satan did was ask Adam and Eve why God would hold them back, keeping them from experiencing all that there was to experience. He planted this seed of an idea that God was fearful of His creation becoming like him.

SMALL GROUP NOTES

Divide the large group into smaller groups of four to six people (depending on the number of facilitators available). Use the questions on page 32 to review the homework from Lesson 1. Then, recite the memory verse from Lesson 1 as a group:

> *In the beginning, God created the heavens and the earth.* —**Genesis 1:1**

Use the questions on pages 32–34 to discuss the main topics from this week's lesson.

Use the following material to help prepare for the discussion time. Read Genesis 3:6 and 1 John 2:15-16 and try to identify what they teach about the nature of temptation. If time allows, also consider reading Matthew 4:1-11.

[Question] What are some ways we experience these kinds of temptations today?

> *[Answer] Remember that Satan was an important part of Adam and Eve's decision to sin.*

[Question] What do John 8:44 and 1 Peter 5:8-9 teach us about Satan?

> *[Answer] These verses teach that Satan can be resisted and defeated.*

[Question] How is Satan different from God?

[Question] How do we see these consequences impacting the world today?

> *[Answer] Adam and Eve were given a choice: believe and obey God, or believe and obey Satan. They chose to believe Satan and disobey God. Their choice resulted in terrible consequences for all people—including death.*

> *We are given the same choice every day. Will we believe and obey God, or will we believe and obey Satan?*

Close the small-group discussion with a time of prayer.

Lesson 2

SIN

LARGE GROUP SESSION

REVIEW LESSON 1

Here are the key topics we covered during our last meeting:

- God is our Creator and Ruler.

- We can learn about God by looking at His creation.

- As our Creator, God has the right to set the rules for His creation.

- All people are created by God, and all people are created to worship Him.

KEY OBJECTIVES

Here are the objectives you'll be discussing in Lesson 2:

- Determine a definition for sin.

- Examine the cause and consequences of our sin.

- Identify Satan's strategy for attacking our weakness so that we will be ready when the attack comes.

SIN

What is sin, and where did it come from?

The Bible is the best place to find answers for life's biggest questions—including sin.

In order to understand sin, we need to understand that everything God created was good in the beginning:

> *And God saw everything that he had made, and behold, it was very good. And there was evening and there was morning, the sixth day.* —**Genesis 1:31**

What would paradise look like for you? Why?

When God created Adam and Eve, the first people, He placed them in a perfect place called the garden of Eden. Adam and Eve had everything they needed—food, fun, easy work, purpose and so on. Best of all, they often spent time in God's presence. They had a perfect relationship with God, each other, and the world.

God only had one rule for Adam and Eve in paradise:

> *The LORD God took the man and put him in the Garden of Eden to work it and keep it. And the LORD God commanded the man, saying, You may surely eat of every tree of the garden, but of the tree of the knowledge of good and evil you shall not eat, for in the day that you eat of it you shall surely die.* —**Genesis 2:15-17**

Do you think this rule was fair? Explain.

Satan tempted Adam and Eve to sin by disobeying God. His main attack was to convince Adam and Eve that God couldn't be trusted and was trying to keep something from them:

> *He [Satan] said to the woman, "Did God actually say, 'You shall not eat of any tree in the garden'?" And the woman said to the serpent, "We may eat*

of the fruit of the trees in the garden, but God
said, 'You shall not eat of the fruit of the tree
that is in the midst of the garden, neither shall
you touch it, lest you die.'" But the serpent said
to the woman, "You will not surely die. For God
knows that when you eat of it your eyes will be
opened, and you will be like God, knowing good
and evil." So when the woman saw that the tree
was good for food, and that it was a delight to the
eyes, and that the tree was to be desired to make
one wise, she took of its fruit and ate, and she
also gave some to her husband who was with her,
and he ate. —**Genesis 3:1-6**

How did Satan get Adam and Eve to doubt God's goodness?

What were some of the reasons why Adam and Eve chose to disobey God?

Adam and Eve's decision to sin brought consequences into their lives—and into the whole world.

To the woman He [God] said, "I will surely mul-
tiply your pain in childbearing; in pain you shall
bring forth children. Your desire shall be contrary
to your husband, but he shall rule over you." And
to Adam He said, "Because you have listened to
the voice of your wife and have eaten of the tree
of which I commanded you, 'You shall not eat of
it,' cursed is the ground because of you; in pain
you shall eat of it all the days of your life; thorns
and thistles it shall bring forth for you; and you
shall eat the plants of the field. By the sweat of
your face you shall eat bread, till you return to

the ground, for out of it you were taken; for you
are dust, and to dust you shall return." —**Genesis**
3:16-19

Where do you see the consequences of sin in the world today?

How have you experienced the consequences of sin in your own life?

Adam and Eve were perfect, but they still sinned against God and experienced major consequences—including physical and spiritual death. The same has been true for every other person throughout the history of the world.

SMALL GROUP SESSION

REVIEW

What did you learn from this week's homework? What questions would you like to ask?

How has what you learned helped you understand God better?

How has what you learned helped you understand yourself better?

Recite the memory verse from Lesson 1:

In the beginning, God created the heavens and
the earth. —**Genesis 1:1**

DISCUSSING SIN

What is sin? Work together as a group to come up with a definition.

What does it mean to be tempted by something?

How does temptation push us toward sin?

Read the following passages and try to identify what they teach about the nature of temptation.

> *So when the woman saw that the tree was good for food, and that it was a delight to the eyes, and that the tree was to be desired to make one wise, she took of its fruit and ate, and she also gave some to her husband who was with her, and he ate.* —**Genesis 3:6**

> *Do not love the world or the things in the world. If anyone loves the world, the love of the Father is not in him. For all that is in the world—**the desires of the flesh and the desires of the eyes and pride of life**—is not from the Father but is from the world.* —**1 John 2:15-16** *(emphasis added)*

How did Adam and Eve experience the following aspects of temptation?

• The desires of the flesh

• The desires of the eyes

• The pride of life

What are some ways we experience these kinds of temptations today?

Who or what is Satan?

> *You are of your father the devil, and your will is to do your father's desires. He was a murderer from the beginning, and does not stand in the truth, because there is no truth in him. When he lies, he speaks out of his own character, for he is a liar and the father of lies.* —**John 8:44**

> *Be sober-minded; be watchful. Your adversary the devil prowls around like a roaring lion, seeking someone to devour. Resist him, firm in your faith, knowing that the same kinds of suffering are being experienced by your brotherhood throughout the world.* —**1 Peter 5:8-9**

What do these verses teach us about Satan?

How is Satan different from God?

Read Genesis 3:14-19 as a group. What were some of the physical consequences of the first sin?

What were some of the spiritual consequences?

How do you see these consequences impacting the world today?

How do we know what God wants us to do each day?

If we're tempted to do something, how can we know whether it's right or wrong?

Where can we get help if we're unsure about something, or if we feel tempted and don't want to sin?

Lesson 2
HOMEWORK

Complete the following assignments before the group gathers for Lesson 3.

Read Genesis 39:7-12 and answer the following questions:

1. How did Joseph experience temptation?

2. How did Joseph respond to temptation?

Read 2 Samuel 11:1-4 and answer the following questions:

1. How did David experience temptation?

2. How did David respond to temptation?

Use the following questions to compare and contrast these two Bible stories.

1. What were the similarities between Joseph and David's temptations?

2. What were the differences between their experiences?

3. What can you apply in your life from their examples?

4. How do Joseph and David illustrate the truth of two paths in life?

Read James 1:14-15. Answer the following questions:

1. Where does temptation come from?

2. What choices do we have when we feel lured or enticed?

3. What are the steps to sin?

4. What is the outcome when we give in to temptation?

Review last week's memory verse:

> *In the beginning, God created the heavens and the earth.* —**Genesis 1:1**

Review this week's memory verse:

> *For all have sinned and fall short of the glory of God.* —**Romans 3:23**

LESSON 3 **MEMORY VERSE**

*For God so loved the world,
that he gave his only Son,
that whoever believes in him
should not perish
but have eternal life.*

John 3:16

Lesson 3 : **Salvation**
FACILITATOR NOTES

KEY TOPICS

- *God has provided for us forgiveness through the death of Jesus Christ on the cross and His resurrection.*
- *God offers salvation to all who will repent and trust in Christ.*
- *Each person must individually respond to God's offer.*

LARGE GROUP NOTES

Begin with an opening prayer before introducing the lesson for the large group. Be sure to conclude the large group portion of your time with a closing prayer.

Using the material on pages 44-47 be sure to introduce the topic. Remember to have all the passages of Scripture read out loud and use this time to identify terms that may be unfamiliar to the men. Here are suggested terms that should be defined (remember to use words that all can understand when defining these terms):

> Iniquity: *A deliberate choice to sin, a willful disobedience to God.*
> Trespass: *You being in a place that you are not allowed to be.*

If time is an issue, the section on Ephesians 2:1-3 can be condensed. Here's how:

Read Ephesians 2:1-3. Summarize what it teaches:

- *We are all born dead in our rebellion and sin, with no spiritual life within us.*
- *We are dominated by evil spiritual forces under Satan whose goal is our destruction.*

- We are doomed to judgment and hell for our rebellion against God.

SMALL GROUP NOTES

Divide the large into smaller groups of four to six people (depending on the number of facilitators available). Use the questions on page 47 to review the homework from Lesson 2.

Recite the memory verses from Lesson 2:

> For all have sinned and fall short of the glory of God. —**Romans 3:23**

Use the material on pages 48-51 to discuss the main topics from this week's lesson. To be raised up with Christ and seated in the heavenlies means that His life is now our life and that His resurrection guarantees our resurrection. Our life is now hid with Christ in God (Colossians 3:1-4). We are now citizens of heaven with Him (Philippians 3:20-21).

Be sure to read together the verses and discuss the questions in this section of the lesson. Be aware that there may be terms in the verses that will need to be defined. Here are some suggested terms needing to be defined in this section (remember to use words that all can understand when defining these terms).

<u>Mercy</u>: God not giving you what you deserve.

<u>Grace</u>: God giving you what you don't deserve.

<u>Justified</u>: God makes you right in His eyes, pronounces you not guilty.

<u>Redemption</u>: God buys you out of slavery and brings you back to Him.

<u>Propitiation</u>: God covers your sin through the sacrifice of Christ and removes His wrath against you and places it on Jesus instead.

Righteousness: God creates a new relationship with us that is built through Jesus.

Repentance: to change our mind about sin and to feel regret and sorrow over our sins and to turn away from sin to God.

Remember to do your best to allow for all to participate in sharing and reading verses.

Recite this week's memory verse:

> For God so loved the world, that he gave his only Son, that whoever believes in him should not perish but have eternal life. **—John 3:16**

Close the small-group discussion with a time of prayer.

Salvation

Lesson 3

SALVATION

LARGE GROUP SESSION

Today we come to the most important lesson in Malachi Dads, the Gospel. The problem is a lot of people have heard the word *gospel* but few people really understand what it means. The word *gospel* actually means good news and the message of the gospel is the good news that God has provided a way to forgive our rebellion and make us His children. So we want to take some time to go over that today.

REVIEW LESSONS 1 & 2

- God is the creator of all things and because He made it, He is in charge of everything. He is sovereign.

- God created everything in the beginning to be very good. The universe and everything in it was perfect, including the first human beings.

- God made human beings in His image. That means we share some things in common with God. What does it mean to be created in His image?

  1. We are personal beings—We have a mind, will, and emotions.

  2. We are relational beings—We were created to have relationships, especially with God.

3. We are religious in nature—We will worship something, either the true God or something less.

And for a time, everything was good. Adam and Eve had a perfect relationship with God, each other and nature. God gave Adam and Eve one rule: don't eat of the fruit of the tree of the knowledge of good and evil or you will surely die. But Satan, himself a rebel against God, tempted Adam and Eve to rebel and violate God's rule and they chose to rebel. As a consequence, Eve would experience pain in childbirth and struggle to take leadership in their relationship. Adam would experience hard labor and toil to provide for his family and there would be futility in his work (thorns and thistles). And for both—they will die physically and return to the dust from which they were taken.

Since all human beings are descended from Adam and Eve, we are all infected with sin and stand guilty before God.

KEY OBJECTIVES

- To understand God's provision for our forgiveness through the death of Jesus Christ on the cross and His resurrection.

- God offers salvation to all who repent and trust in Christ.

- Each person must individually respond to God's offer.

SALVATION

When did you break something valuable as a kid? What happened next?

We broke our relationship with God when we rebelled and now we are living with the consequences. Our dilemma is that we are made for a relationship with God, but our sin has separated us from Him and makes that impossible.

But your iniquities have made a separation between you and your God, and your sins have hidden his face from you so that he does not hear. —**Isaiah 59:2**

What does Isaiah tell us about the consequences of our sin?

How does God punish our sin (and remain just and holy) but pardon us (demonstrating His grace and mercy)? Paul lays out mankind's dilemma and God's solution in Ephesians 2.

OUR PROBLEM

And you were dead in the trespasses and sins, in which you once walked, following the course of this world. —**Ephesians 2:1-2a**

How does Paul describe our spiritual condition apart from Christ?

How many times do you have to kick a corpse before it gets up and moves?

So sin has made us spiritually dead and unable to have a relationship with God.

Following the prince of the power of the air, the spirit that is now at work in the sons of disobedience. Among whom we all once lived in the passions of our flesh, carrying out the desires of the body and the mind. —**Ephesians 2:2b-3a**

When we live without Christ, whose power dominates us?

How widespread is Satan's influence?

Where have you experienced the influence of Satan in a harmful way?

> *You are of your father the devil, and your will is to do your father's desires. He was a murderer from the beginning, and he has nothing to do with the truth because there is no truth in him. Whenever he lies, he speaks out of his own character, for he is a liar and the father of lies.* —**John 8:44**

> *The thief comes only to kill and steal and destroy.* —**John 10:10a**

What do these verses teach us about Satan?

So on our own we are under the domination of Satan, whose desire is to kill us and destroy us, and he uses lies and deception to do it.

> *And were by nature, children of wrath, like the rest of mankind.* —**Ephesians 2:3b**

What does it mean to be a child of wrath?

Left to ourselves we are doomed, destined for God's judgment for our sin and rebellion against God and left with no way out.

CONSEQUENCES

> *For all have sinned and fall short of the glory of God.* —**Romans 3:23**

> *The wages of sin is death.* —**Romans 6:23a**

What is a wage? What do these verses teach us about the consequences of sin?

Every human being ever born is born spiritually dead in their sin and faces judgment for their rebellion against God.

Putting all these together, we are hopeless. We are dead in our sins with no real life in us and no relationship with God. We live under the domination of Satan and his minions who use lies and deception to deceive and destroy us. And we are doomed, destined for judgment and hell because of our rebellion against God. On our own we have no hope. But fortunately, God did not leave us on our own.

SMALL GROUP SESSION

REVIEW

What did you learn from last week's homework? What questions would you like to ask?

How has what you learned helped you understand God better?

How has what you learned helped you understand yourself better?

Recite the memory verses from Lessons 1 and 2:

> *In the beginning, God created the heavens and the earth.* —**Genesis 1:1**

> *For all have sinned and fall short of the glory of God.* —**Romans 3:23**

SALVATION – GOD'S ANSWER

But God, being rich in mercy, because of the great love with which he loved us. —**Ephesians 2:4**

How do those words *But God* make you feel?

Notice how Paul describes God. He is not just merciful, He's rich in mercy; He doesn't just love us; He loves us with a great love.

Even when we were dead in our trespasses, made us alive together with Christ—by grace you have been saved—and raised us up with him and seated us with him in the heavenly places in Christ Jesus. —**Ephesians 2:5-6**

Our greatest need was for spiritual life and God has given it to us through the death and resurrection of His Son, Jesus Christ.

What does it mean to be raised up with Him and seated in the heavenly places?

So that in the coming ages he might show the immeasurable riches of his grace in kindness toward us in Christ Jesus. —**Ephesians 2:7**

What picture does this verse bring to your mind?

Because God has raised us up through His grace in Jesus Christ, He wants to display us as trophies of His grace for all eternity. If God had a cell phone, your picture would be in it. Why? Because He is rich in mercy and loves us with a great love.

For by grace you have been saved through faith. And this not your own doing; it is a gift of God;

not as a result of works so that no one may boast.
—**Ephesians 2:8-9**

What part do our works play in salvation?

What is a gift?

What is the best gift you have ever received?

It's all a gift of God's grace from start to finish. We can't earn it; we don't deserve it; God gives us forgiveness and eternal life because of His rich mercy and great love. Even the faith to believe is a gift of His grace.

DISCUSSION

Before God could save us from our sins, our sins had to be duly punished. How did God do that? There are 3 great Christian words that describe what God has done for us: justification, redemption and propitiation. Each tells us something about salvation.

> *. . .and are justified by His grace as a gift, through the redemption that is in Christ Jesus, whom God put forward as a propitiation by His blood.* —**Romans 3:24-25**

> *Therefore, since we have been justified by faith, we have peace with God through our Lord Jesus Christ.* —**Romans 5:1**

What would it mean to be justified in a human courtroom? What does it mean to be justified before God?

Justified means to be declared not guilty by God and treated as if we had never sinned.

In him we have redemption through his blood, the forgiveness of our trespasses, according to the riches of his grace. —**Ephesians 1:7**

What does it mean to redeem something?

How does God redeem us?

Redemption means to be bought out of slavery through the payment of a price, in our case the blood of Christ shed on the cross for our sins.

...and are justified by his grace as a gift, through the redemption that is in Christ Jesus, whom God put forward as a propitiation by his blood, to be received by faith. —**Romans 3:24-25**

A propitiation is a sacrifice that covers sin and turns God's wrath and judgment away from us. Thanks to Christ's death on the cross, our sins were punished in Jesus, God's wrath was poured out on His Son, and our sins are covered by His blood. He bore our guilt and punishment so that we could receive God's forgiveness and new life.

Justification, redemption and propitiation sum up what God has done for us through the death of Jesus Christ on the cross. His death covers our sin and removes God judgment from us; he took our punishment, allowing God to declare us not guilty, and He paid the price in His blood to buy us out of slavery to sin.

Which of these words means the most to you?

> *For our sake he made him to be sin who knew no sin, so that in him we might become the righteousness of God.* —**2 Corinthians 5:21**

What did Christ do for us in this verse? What did He give us in exchange?

This verse is called the great exchange. God took all our sin and the judgment it deserved and put it on Christ on the cross and punished it there. Then God took the perfect righteousness and obedience of Christ and put it on us. God put our sin on Christ, treated Him like He was us, and then He put the perfect righteousness of Christ on us and treats us like we are Him.

But it's not enough to simply know these truths, we must respond to them. Each person must individually place his trust in Christ.

> *But to all who did receive him, who believed in his name, he gave the right to become children of God.* —**John 1:12**

> *Because if you confess with your mouth that Jesus is Lord and believe in your heart God raised him from the dead, you will be saved.* —**Romans 10:9**

> *Believe in the Lord Jesus Christ and you shall be saved.* —**Acts 16:31**

> *Repent and believe the gospel.* —**Mark 1:15b**

To repent means to change your mind about sin, to feel regret and sorrow over it, and to turn away from sin and turn to God.

PRAYER OF SALVATION

Dear God in heaven, I come to You in the name of Jesus. I acknowledge to You that I am a sinner and I am sorry for my sins and the life I've lived. I need Your forgiveness.

I believe that Your only begotten Son, Jesus Christ, shed His precious blood on the cross and died for my sins.

You say in Your holy word, in Romans 10:9, that if we confess that Jesus Christ is our Lord, and believe in our hearts that You raised Him from the dead, we shall be saved.

Right now I confess that Jesus Christ is my Savior. With my heart, I believe that You raised Him from the dead. This very moment I accept Jesus Christ as my Lord and Savior and surrender to Him. According to Your word, right now I am saved.

I thank You Jesus for Your abundant grace, which has saved me from judgment for my sins. I thank You Jesus that Your grace never leads to more sin but rather always leads to repentance. Therefore Lord Jesus, transform my life so that I may bring glory and honor to You alone and not to myself.

Thank You for dying for me and giving me eternal life. Amen.

Name: _____

Date: _____

Lesson 3
HOMEWORK

Complete the following assignments before the group gathers for Lesson 4. The Bible uses a number of different words to describe what God means by salvation. Each word gives a different glimpse into what full salvation involves. We looked at justification, redemption and propitiation already. Now let's look at three more.

Adoption – Read Ephesians 1:5-6 and Romans 8:14-17.

1. What do you think of when you hear the word *adoption*?

2. Does it matter if God adopts us as His sons? How does that change our relationship with God?

3. When have you sensed that the Holy Spirit has borne witness in you that you are indeed a child of God?

Reconciliation – Read 2 Corinthians 5:18-19.

1. Why did we need reconciliation with God?

2. What caused our war with God?

3. How did God make peace with us?

Transferred – Read Colossians 1:13-14 and John 8:44.

1. What was the kingdom like that we were part of? Who ruled it? What is he like?

2. What is the Kingdom like that we are now part of? Who rules it? What is He like?

3. What made it possible to be transferred from the kingdom of darkness to the kingdom of light?

Review this week's memory verse:

> For God so loved the world, that he gave his only Son, that whoever believes in him should not perish but have eternal life. —**John 3:16**

LESSON 4 **MEMORY VERSE**

And I will give you a new heart,
and a new spirit I will put within you.
And I will remove the heart of stone from your
flesh and give you a heart of flesh.

Ezekiel 36:26

Lesson 4 : **Christian Living — Part One**
FACILITATOR NOTES

KEY TOPICS

• *When we make a commitment to Christ, God acts to transform us.*

• *God gives us a new heart, making us spiritually alive. We are new creations.*

• *God gives us His power, sending His Holy Spirit to live within us so we can obey Him.*

• *We need to begin to walk in the power of the Spirit.*

LARGE GROUP NOTES

Begin with an opening prayer before introducing the lesson for the large group.

Be sure to conclude the large group portion of your time with a closing prayer.

Use the material on pages 62-65 to be sure to introduce the topic. Remember to have all the passages of Scripture read out loud and use this time to identify terms that may be unfamiliar to the men.

Be sure to emphasize the truth of God's holiness and His expectation and desire to see His children follow after Christ's example. The tension comes from the fact that as sinners corrupted by sin we are unable to meet this expectation and are unable to ever measure up to God's standard. Yet, God is merciful and provides a way for us to be set free from sin's control by giving us a new heart and His power to stand against sin once we are saved through Jesus Christ.

Make sure that your group understands the awesome reality in Christ that they are "new" and that the "old" is gone.

Remember that the word heart is used in the Scriptures to describe a person's identity and character... the DNA of what makes a person unique.

The power against sin's control in the life of a believer comes from God alone through the presence of the Holy Spirit. Focus on this fact: Alone we are powerless against sin. We will continue to fall under temptations and the pressures of the world. God's goodness toward His children is that we are not alone and that because of the Spirit's living inside of us we have the ability with a new heart to say no to the temptations that come our way.

Success in Christian living (the process of sanctification) comes through obedience to God's Word and living under the power of the Holy Spirit.

SMALL GROUP NOTES

Divide the large group into smaller groups of four to six people (depending on the number of facilitators available). Use the questions on page 66 to review the homework from Lesson 3.

Recite the memory verse from Lesson 3:

> For God so loved the world, that he gave his only Son, that whoever believes in him should not perish but have eternal life. —**John 3:16**

Use the material on pages 66-69 to discuss the main topics from this week's lesson. Be sure to read together the verses and discuss the questions in this section of the lesson. Be aware that there may be terms in the verses that will need to be defined. Here are some suggested terms and concepts needing to be defined and discussed in this section (remember to use words that all can understand when defining these terms).

- Walk: A description of a person's lifestyle. (Make sure to underscore the difference from a mistake that leads to a sin compared to a habit that is ongoing. Your walk is your "normal" pattern of life.)

- A short explanation for: "being transformed into the same image from one degree of glory to another" (2 Corinthians 3:18). Believers are being changed (transformed) from one lifestyle (image) that followed the world to a better one by following the lifestyle modeled by Jesus. This glory is the new character Christians receive from God.

- Take some time to focus on the "putting off" and "putting on" from Ephesians 4:22-23, make sure that your small group can see the difference in these actions. Understand that this is the responsibility of the believer in obedience to put on the new self, daily. It is a choice that you have to make.

Remember to do your best to allow for all to participate in sharing and reading verses.

Recite this week's memory verse:

> And I will give you a new heart, and a new spirit I will put within you. And I will remove the heart of stone from your flesh and give you a heart of flesh. —**Ezekiel 36:26**

Close the small-group discussion with a time of prayer.

Lesson 4

CHRISTIAN LIVING
PART 1

LARGE GROUP SESSION

In today's lesson we will focus our attention on a very important topic. After last week's lesson where we looked at the gospel and what it means to become a follower of Jesus, we now turn our attention to how to practically live for Jesus in this new life. This new life is a process that is called sanctification. We will look at two aspects of sanctification: what part God has in growing you in your faith and what part you have in maturing your faith.

REVIEW LESSON 3

- God has provided for us forgiveness through the death of Jesus Christ on the cross and His resurrection.

- God offers salvation to all who will repent and trust in Christ.

- Each person must individually respond to God's offer.

The story of the gospel is a story of God's goodness to all those that are under the curse of the fall. It is because of the great mercy of God that there is hope that all sins can be forgiven, and our relationship with God will be restored. All of this happens only because of the gift of Jesus and His sacrifice on the cross.

*For there is salvation in no one else, for there is
no other name under heaven given among men by
which we must be saved.* —**Acts 4:12**

KEY OBJECTIVES

- When we make a commitment to Christ, God acts to transform us.

- God gives us a new heart, making us spiritually alive. We are new creations.

- God gives us His power, sending His Holy Spirit to live within us so we can obey Him.

- We need to begin to walk in the power of the Spirit.

DISCUSSION – CHRISTIAN LIVING

To start our time together we will look at two aspects of sanctification that God is involved in. The first thing that God does for those that have been saved is He begins to make changes in His children. Once we are adopted into the family of God through the work of Jesus, God starts to recreate us to be more like Jesus. These changes are a work that only God can do. These changes are part of sanctification.

God is perfect and holy; He desires that all who follow Him be like Him. This should be the goal for all Christians. Each day is another opportunity to take another step of faithfulness to God in obedience.

What are some of the hopes you have for your children?

What type of person would you like your child to become?

*As obedient children, do not be conformed to
the passions of your former ignorance, but as he
who called you is holy, you also be holy in all your
conduct.* —**1 Peter 1:14-15**

*You therefore must be perfect, as your heavenly
Father is perfect.* —**Matthew 5:48**

If you had the power to change something in your life what would change?

Unlike you and me, God does have the power to make changes in those who surrender to Him. He is able to fix what is broken in all of us.

*Therefore, if anyone is in Christ, he is a new cre-
ation. The old has passed away; behold, the new
has come.* —**2 Corinthians 5:17**

How would you describe the "old" and the "new" in your life?

What are the differences between the "old" and the "new"?

What do you think it means to be a new creation?

So how does God make us a new creation? He does it by changing our heart. The old heart was corrupted by sin. Remember last week we saw from the Scriptures, that before Christ we are all influenced by Satan and the things of this world. Before salvation we were all slaves to sin, we could not help but do what is evil in God's eyes. God needed to rebuild what was broken in our lives. He does this by taking out what is broken and putting in a new part. This new part He puts into a believer is a new heart.

*And I will give you a new heart, and a new spirit
I will put within you, And I will remove the heart
of stone from your flesh and give you a heart of
flesh. And I will put my Spirit within you, and
cause you to walk in my statutes and be careful
to obey my rules.* —**Ezekiel 36:26-27**

In the Scriptures the heart isn't just the organ that moves your
blood throughout your body. The idea of "heart" centers more on
what makes someone a person. It's your identity, your character.
Your heart is what makes YOU, you. And that is what God changes.
At salvation he takes the old you that is full of rebellion and sin and
changes you so that you can now grow and change and follow Him.
You can now have the desire to follow Him and live the way He
designed you to live.

Why is a "heart of stone" a bad thing in God's eyes?

Have you been given a new heart by God?

What are some indications that God has changed your heart?

A heart of flesh can grow. It is able to change. Only when we have
a soft heart to God are we able to become more like Jesus. If we
have a heart of stone, we are unable to change. We are stuck and
dead to what God can do.

Now a believer in Christ Jesus who has a new heart can say "yes"
to Him and "no" to the things of the world that take you away from
Jesus. You have been given the power in Christ to say no to sin.

*His divine power has granted to us all things that
pertain to life and godliness, through the knowledge of him who called us to his own glory and
excellence.* —**2 Peter 1:3**

This power that is now available to a believer to say no to sin and walk in obedience to God comes from the presence of the Holy Spirit. As we live from day to day and year to year, we slowly become more and more like Jesus because of His presence and power in our life.

> But you will receive power when the Holy Spirit
> has come upon you, and you will be my witnesses
> in Jerusalem and in all Judea and Samaria, and
> to the end of the earth. —**Acts 1:8**

Describe a time where you have seen the power of God in your life when He helped you say no to sin and yes to Him.

These changes that God makes in our life are the first steps towards becoming more and more like Jesus. The process of change is what sanctification is about. A simple definition for sanctification is: *God working with you to make you look more like Jesus day by day*. God wants us to become better versions of ourselves by becoming more like Jesus.

> Therefore, my beloved, as you have always
> obeyed, so now, not only as in my presence but
> much more in my absence, work out your own
> salvation with fear and trembling, for it is God
> who works in you, both to will and to work for his
> good pleasure. —**Philippians 2:12-13**

Why do you think God wants us to be more like Jesus?

Can you think of something that you can do this week that will help you be more like Jesus?

SMALL GROUP SESSION

REVIEW

What did you learn from this week's homework? What questions would you like to ask?

How has what you learned helped you understand God better?

How has what you learned helped you understand yourself better?

Recite the memory verse from Lesson 3:

> *For God so loved the world, that he gave his only Son, that whoever believes in him should not perish but have eternal life.* —**John 3:16**

DISCUSSION — CHRISTIAN LIVING

God has big plans for His children as they grow in relationship with Him. In this lesson on sanctification, we have discussed how God changes us over time to be more and more like Jesus so that we can be faithful to Him. Believers are being changed for a purpose. God has a plan and a purpose for each of His children and has created each to accomplish His work.

> *For we are his workmanship, created in Christ Jesus for good works, which God prepared beforehand, that we should walk in them.* —**Ephesians 2:10**

What type of works do you think God has in store for you to do?

Are you ready to do what God created you to do?

In the Scriptures the word for *walk* can be understood to describe someone's lifestyle. It has to do with one's conduct and integrity. In order to do the work that God has created for His children, He expects His children to walk a lifestyle that honors Him.

> *We exhorted each one of you and encouraged you and charged you to walk in a manner worthy of God, who calls you into his own kingdom and glory.* —**1 Thessalonians 2:12**

> *I therefore, a prisoner for the Lord, urge you to walk in a manner worthy of the calling to which you have been called.* —**Ephesians 4:1**

Would you say that your "walk" has been all that God would want it to be?

Understand that to be able to "walk" in a way that pleases God can only happen when Christians rely on the power of God. Without God's provision and grace to live the life He desires for His children there is no way for humans to succeed. As was talked about in the last chapter, all human beings "have sinned and fall short of the glory of God" (Romans 3:23).

> *But I say, walk by the Spirit, and you will not gratify the desires of the flesh. For the desires of the flesh are against the Spirit, and the desires of the Spirit are against the flesh, for these are opposed to each other, to keep you from doing the things you want to do.* —**Galatians 5:16-17**

It is only when believers walk in the power of the Spirit that they have victory over those things that lead to sin.

Why would God, as your heavenly Father, be concerned with how you live your life?

God is such a wonderful and gracious Father who provides for His children by giving us new life in Christ. He not only changes us by putting a new heart in believers and by providing the power to stand against the temptations of sin, He also sends us a Helper so that we are not alone in this new life that He has given to us. This Helper is the Holy Spirit who helps us live the life God calls each of His children to live.

Part of sanctification is also the responsibility of the Christian. Though God does so much for us so we can live for Him, He still requires His children to be faithful to Him.

> But the fruit of the Spirit is love, joy, peace, patience, kindness, goodness, faithfulness, gentleness, self-control; against such things there is no law. —**Galatians 5:22-23**

A fruit tree can grow fruit. Everything is there in the tree for the fruit to grow. At the right time the flowers come; these flowers then change into baby, immature fruit. The fruit is there, it's just not ripe or mature yet; that too takes time. This is what the Holy Spirit does for the believer. All the potential of the fruit of the Spirit is there in the life of a believer. It takes time and faithfulness to ripen the fruit. Your part as a believer is being faithful to mature this fruit in your life.

Which fruit of the Spirit do you need to cultivate more in your life? Why?

Which fruit of the Spirit do you see maturing in your life?

We need to understand that sanctification is a gradual process. As we live from day to day and year to year, we slowly become more and more like Jesus. Like we said before, the Holy Spirit is deeply involved in this process:

> And we all, with unveiled face, beholding the

glory of the Lord, are being transformed into the
same image from one degree of glory to another.
For this comes from the Lord who is the Spirit.
—2 Corinthians 3:18

We also must choose each day to reject our old, sinful ways of doing things. Instead, we must choose to follow Christ by "putting on" the new person He's made us.

> *…to put off your old self, which belongs to your*
> *former manner of life and is corrupt through*
> *deceitful desires, and to be renewed in the spirit*
> *of your minds, and to put on the new self, created*
> *after the likeness of God in true righteousness*
> *and holiness.* **—Ephesians 4:22-24**

What are two things that you can do this week that you can "put off"?

SUMMARY

- God helps believers in their sanctification by putting a new heart in them and taking away the heart of stone.

- God helps by giving believers the power to stand against the world and temptation.

- God sends the Holy Spirit to help believers walk in obedience and faithfulness.

This Week's Memory Verse:

> *And I will give you a new heart, and a new spirit*
> *I will put within you. And I will remove the heart*
> *of stone from your flesh and give you a heart of*
> *flesh.* **—Ezekiel 36:26**

LESSON 4
HOMEWORK

Complete the following assignments before the group gathers for Lesson 5.

Read Romans 12:9-21, then answer the following questions.

1. What do you like best about these verses? Why?

2. What do you find most challenging about these verses? Why?

3. Where will you find help and support to live the kind of life described in these verses?

Read Ephesians 4:20-32, then answer the following questions.

1. Why should you put off your old self?

2. What are some actions we are to put off?

3. What are some actions we are to put on?

Read Ephesians 5:1-2,15-16, then answer the following questions.

1. What is one way you can be an imitator of God?

2. What example does Paul give in verse 2 for walking in love? Why should you walk in love?

3. How can you become wise? How does wisdom affect your life?

4. What are some ways that you can better use your time to honor God?

Read Galatians 5:19-24, then answer the following questions.

1. List out the works of the flesh found in verses 19-21. Which ones in that list do you currently struggle with?

2. What do you see as the source that drives the need to do the works of the flesh?

3. List out the fruit of the Spirit in verses 22-24. Which ones in that list do you currently see developing in your life?

4. What characteristic from the list of the fruit of the Spirit do you presently struggle with in maturing? Why?

LESSON 5 **MEMORY VERSE**

Work out your own salvation with fear and trembling, for it is God who works in you, both to will and to work for his good pleasure.

Philippians 2:12b-13

Lesson 5 : **Christian Living — Part 2**
FACILITATOR NOTES

KEY TOPICS

• *We are to cooperate with God in growing in our Christian faith.*

• *To grow spiritually, we need to become men of the book, studying and applying the Bible to our lives. It is God's owner's manual for human beings.*

• *To grow spiritually, we have to talk to our Father. We do that through prayer.*

• *To grow spiritually, we need to be part of God's family, the local church.*

LARGE GROUP NOTES

Begin with prayer Show the men the role they have in their Christian growth. We are to cooperate with God.

Use this section to introduce the truth that to grow spiritually, we must study the Bible, talk to our Father in prayer, and be part of a church family.

SMALL GROUP NOTES

Divide into small groups. Use the questions on pages 80–81 to review the homework from lesson 4.

Recite the memory verse from Lesson 4:

> *And I will give you a new heart, and a new spirit I will put within you. And I will remove the heart of stone from your flesh and give you a heart of flesh.* **—Ezekiel 36:26**

Use the material on pages 81–86 to go deeper into the reason why studying the Bible, praying to our Father, and being part of a church family are essential to grow as Christians. Be sure to emphasize that we have to do our part if we want to grow as Christians. Christian growth is not automatic but comes as we grow in the knowledge of God and learn to walk by His Spirit day to day.

Being men of the book is critical to growing as Christians. We need a plan for regular Bible reading and study to grow. Share what works for you.

We need to develop the habit of talking with our Father daily in prayer. If you have a particular way you do that, share that with the men. ACTS (Adoration, Confession, Thanksgiving, and Supplication) is one formula.

Christians can't grow in isolation from other believers. We were created to be part of the church family. Look for ways to share how your church is a blessing to you.

Recite this week's memory verse:

> *Work out your own salvation with fear and trembling, for it is God who works in you, both to will and to work for his good pleasure.* —**Philippians 2:12b-13**

Close the small group time in prayer.

CHRISTIAN LIVING
PART 2

LARGE GROUP SESSION

REVIEW LESSON 4

- When we make a commitment to Christ, God acts to transform us.

- God gives us a new heart, making us spiritually alive. We are new creations.

- God gives us His power, sending His Holy Spirit to lives within us so we can obey Him.

- We need to begin to walk in the power of the Spirit.

KEY OBJECTIVES

- While God has given us a new heart and given us His Spirit, we have a responsibility too.

- We are to cooperate with God in growing in our Christian faith.

- To grow spiritually, we need to become men of the book, studying and applying the Bible to our lives. It is God's owner's manual for human beings.

- To grow spiritually, we have to talk to our heavenly Father. We do that through prayer.

- To grow spiritually, we need to be part of God's family, the local church.

COOPERATION

Describe a time when you cooperated with other people to achieve a goal.

While salvation is all God's work by grace through faith, spiritual growth involves our cooperation with God. The process of sanctification, becoming more like Jesus every day, involves us doing our part to cooperate with God in our growth.

> *Therefore, my beloved, as you have always obeyed, so now, not only as in my presence but much more in my absence, work out your own salvation with fear and trembling, for it is God who works in you, both to will and to work for his good pleasure.* —**Philippians 2:12-13**

What do these verses tell us about the Christian life?

How do we work out our salvation with fear and trembling?

THE BIBLE

It is impossible to follow Jesus if we don't know what Jesus wants for us. God has given us the Bible as an owner's manual for human beings. In it, God tells us what He expects from His children.

Why is it important to read the owner's manual for a car or power tool? What can happen if we don't?

God has given us His word, the Bible, to get us ready to serve Him.

> *Like newborn infants, long for the pure spiritual milk, that by it you may grow up into salvation.*
> —**1 Peter 2:2**

How much do newborn infants long for their mother's milk?

The Bible is the pure spiritual milk for all Christians. Without a steady diet of the Bible, we can't grow spiritually.

PRAYER – TALKING TO OUR FATHER

You can't have a relationship with someone without communicating with them. God speaks to us through the Bible and His Spirit. We speak to God through prayer.

> *But you have received the Spirit of adoption as sons, by whom we cry, 'Abba! Father!' The Spirit bears witness with our spirit that we are children of God.* —**Romans 8:15b-16**
>
> *Pray then like this: "Our Father in heaven...."*
> —**Matthew 6:9**

What picture does the Bible use to describe our relationship with God?

How should this affect our view of prayer?

OUR FAMILY: THE CHURCH

The final way we grow spiritually is by becoming part of God's family, the church. A child without a family is an orphan. That's why God wants all His sons to become part of His local family, the church.

> So those who received his (Peter's) word were baptized, and there were added that day about three thousand souls. —**Acts 2:41**

On the day the church started, 3,000 people believed the message Peter preached. But they weren't left to fend for themselves. They were added to the fellowship of the church. The first step was that they were baptized in water as a sign of their conversion and incorporation into the church. The verses that follow tell what these first Christians did when they were together.

> And they devoted themselves to the apostles' teaching and the fellowship, to the breaking of bread and the prayers And day by day, attending the temple together and breaking bread in their homes, they received their food with glad and generous hearts. —**Acts 2:42, 46**

How did these first Christians live their lives?

What stands out to you in these verses?

SMALL GROUP SESSION

REVIEW

What did you learn from this week's homework? What questions would you like to ask?

How has it helped you understand God better?

How has what you learned helped you understand yourself better?

Recite the memory verse from Lesson 4:

> And I will give you a new heart, and a new spirit
> I will put within you. And I will remove the heart
> of stone from your flesh and give you a heart of
> flesh. —**Ezekiel 36:26**

DISCUSSING THE BIBLE

Because the Bible is the owner's manual for human beings, we are exhorted over and over again to be men of the book. We can't obey God if we don't know what He wants us to do. It starts with renewing our minds.

> I appeal to you therefore, brothers, by the mer-
> cies of God, to present your bodies to God as
> a living sacrifice, holy and acceptable to God,
> which is your spiritual worship. Do not be con-
> formed to this world, but be transformed by the
> renewal of your mind, that by testing you may
> discern what is the will of God, what is good and
> acceptable and perfect. —**Romans 12:1-2**

Before we can live as God wants us to, we have to begin to think like God wants us to think. That means we have to renew our minds. The way God renews our minds is through the truth of His word.

What does God promise we will learn when we allow Him to transform our minds?

Let's look at why the Bible matters.

> All Scripture is breathed out by God and profit-
> able for teaching, for reproof, for correction, and
> for training in righteousness, that the man of God
> may be complete, equipped for every good work.
> —**2 Timothy 3:16-17**

According to Paul, who wrote the Bible?

What ways does God use the Bible to grow us up as Christians?

What is the ultimate goal for how God uses His Word in our lives?

> Blessed is the man who walks not in the counsel
> of the wicked, nor stands in the way of sinners,
> nor sits in the seat of scoffers; but his delight is
> in the law of the Lord, and on his law he medi-
> tates day and night. He is like a tree planted by
> streams of water that yields its fruit in its season,
> and its leaf does not wither. In all he does, he
> prospers. —**Psalm 1:1-3**

God lays out for us what it means to be a blessed man. First, the
blessed man is careful to avoid certain things.

What does the man who wants to be blessed have to avoid?

Then the blessed man must commit himself to certain things.

What must the blessed man put his time and energy into?

**What does it mean to meditate on God's Word? What are some
practical ways of doing that?**

What is David trying to tell us by the picture of a tree planted by streams of water?

DISCUSSING PRAYER

One of the great privileges God gives us as His children is the privilege of having a relationship with Him through prayer. As we saw earlier, God invites us to pray to Him as our Abba (Daddy). Let's look at some truths about prayer.

> *And when you pray, you must not be like the hypocrites. For they love to stand and pray in the synagogues and at the street corners, that they may be seen by others.... But when you pray, go into your room and shut the door and pray to your Father who is in secret. And your Father who sees in secret will reward you.* —**Matthew 6:5-6**

What does Jesus warn us about here? When should our most sincere prayers be prayed?

> *And when you pray, do not heap up empty phrases as the Gentiles do, for they think that they will be heard for their many words. Do not be like them because your Father knows what you need before you ask him.* —**Matthew 6:7-8**

What does Jesus warn us against in these verses?

Why do we not have to impress God with the amount of words we pray?

Jewish religious leaders loved to pray in front of people at the synagogue and in public. Gentiles thought if they heaped up enough words, they could wear God down and He would give them what they wanted. When we pray, we are coming to our Father who knows what we need and loves us and we are laying our needs before Him. It's not the words we pray that impress God but the heart behind them. God hears our heart, not our words.

> *Do not be anxious about anything, but in every-*
> *thing by prayer and supplication let your requests*
> *be made known to God. And the peace of God*
> *which surpasses all understanding, will guard*
> *your hearts and minds in Christ Jesus.*
> **—Philippians 4:6-7**

What kinds of things can we bring to God in prayer?

How can praying to God make us less anxious? When have you experienced God's peace after praying?

DISCUSSING THE CHURCH

When most people think of a church, they think of a building. But in the New Testament, the church isn't a building; they didn't have any. The church is the people, believing Christians who gathered together for teaching, worship, prayer, and fellowship. The church isn't optional for Christians, it's critical if we ever want to grow as followers of Christ.

The book of Hebrews makes several valuable points about why the church should matter to all of us.

> *But exhort one another every day, as long it is*
> *called "today," that none of you may be hardened*
> *by the deceitfulness of sin.* **—Hebrews 3:13**

Why do we need to be close to other Christians? How often are we to stay close to other Christians?

What does sin try to do to us every day?

When is a time when a friend has warned you of something dangerous?

> *And let us consider how to stir up one another*
> *to love and good works, not neglecting to meet*
> *together, as is the habit of some, but encouraging*
> *one another, and all the more as you see the Day*
> *drawing near.* —**Hebrews 10:24-25**

What should we be doing when we gather as brothers in Christ?

What does it mean to stir one another up to love and good works? How do we do that?

Jesus has provided His church with leaders to help believers grow.

> *Obey your leaders and submit to them, for they*
> *are keeping watch over your souls, as those who*
> *will have to give an account. Let them do this*
> *with joy and not with groaning, for that would be*
> *of no advantage to you.* —**Hebrews 13:17**

Why has God put spiritual leaders (pastors, elders, and deacons) in our lives? What should our attitude toward them be?

> *And He (God) gave the apostles, the prophets,*
> *the evangelists, the shepherds and teachers, to*
> *equip the saints for the work of ministry.*
> —**Ephesians 4:11-12**

What are church leaders to do? What are they to equip believers to do?

If we are outside the fellowship of the church, then we have no shepherds to watch over us and equip us and guide us. Satan's first target is always the lone sheep on his own. We need a local church that can help us grow in our faith.

Jesus has given the church a mandate on what we are to do together until He returns.

> And Jesus came and said to them, "All authority in heaven and on earth has been given to me. Go therefore and make disciples of all nations, baptizing them in the name of the Father and of the Son and of the Holy Spirit, teaching them to observe all that I have commanded you. And behold, I am with you always, to the end of the age. —**Matthew 28:18-20**

As the church, what are believers commanded to do?

How do we make disciples?

Finally, believers are given a number of commands in the New Testament that believers are to obey. But many of them cannot be obeyed apart from other believers:

- Love one another.
- Encourage one another.
- Exhort one another.
- Comfort one another.
- Serve one another.

All of these commands need the fellowship of the church to be obeyed. Believers cannot serve Christ faithfully without the fellowship of other believers.

SUMMARY

• Growing as a Christian involves our cooperation with God.

• We must be men of the book who spend time reading and studying God's owner's manual, the Bible.

• We have to talk with our heavenly Father through prayer.

• As God's sons, we need to be involved in a spiritual family, the church.

Lesson 5

HOMEWORK

Complete the following assignments before the group gathers for Lesson 6.

God has given us the Bible so we can live lives that please Him.

> *I have stored up your word in my heart, that I might not sin against you.* —**Psalm 119:11**

1. What does it mean to store up God's Word in our hearts?

2. What are some practical ways to memorize Scripture?

To grow as Christians, we need to learn to talk to our Father.

Pray without ceasing. **—1 Thessalonians 5:17**

Praying at all times in the Spirit, with all prayer and supplication. To that end keep alert with all perseverance, making supplication for all the saints. **—Ephesians 6:18**

1. What does it mean to pray without ceasing?

2. How do we allow the Holy Spirit to help direct our prayers?

3. What can help us stay alert and persevere in our prayer to God?

4. Who should we be praying for in our prayers?

To grow as Christians we need to learn what our spiritual gifts are and use them in serving our brothers and sisters in our church family. We all have a spiritual gift.

Having gifts that differ according to the grace given to us, let us use them. **—Romans 12:6**

As each has received a gift, use it to serve one another, as good stewards of God's varied grace. **—1 Peter 4:10**

1. Where do spiritual gifts come from? What are we to do with our gifts?

2. What does Peter mean when he tells us to be good stewards?

A steward was the person who managed someone else's resources. He wasn't the owner, but the one who was to put the resources to work for the good of his master. For example, Joseph was the steward for Potiphar in the book of Genesis. We are stewards of the spiritual gifts God has given us.

Review this week's memory verse:

> *Work out your own salvation with fear and trembling, for it is God who works in you, both to will and to work for his good pleasure.* —**Philippians 2:12b-13**

LESSON 6 **MEMORY VERSE**

*Therefore a man shall leave his father
and his mother and hold fast to his wife,
and they shall become one flesh.*

Genesis 2:24

Lesson 6 : **Marriage — Part 1**
FACILITATOR NOTES

KEY TOPICS

• *Identify the origin of marriage.*

• *Explore the problems sin caused for marriage.*

• *Understand the biblical reasons for marriage.*

LARGE GROUP NOTES

Begin with an opening prayer. Use the questions on pages 98–100 to begin addressing the topic of marriage according to God's Word. When God created Eve and brought her to Adam, He gave away the first bride.

The idea of male and female means God created two complimentary sexes, who together reflect the fullness of the image of God in mankind. Each reflects different aspects of God's image. Neither is more valuable or important than the other. Both are image bearers.

The fact that Adam and Eve were naked and unashamed tells us that they were completely open and transparent with each other and had nothing to hide. It was only after sin entered their relationship that they felt the need to hide from God and one another.

THE MALACHI DADS PLEDGE

Recite the pledge together as a group:

> *As a Malachi Dad, I solemnly pledge to glorify God and build His Kingdom by prioritizing the raising of godly children first in my family, then in the influencing of other men to do the same in theirs. I firmly believe that my transformed life in Christ—my*

life of integrity, pursuit of this vision, and the pursuit of godly character—will allow me to impact my children, family, and others towards this end.

I will practice a life of daily discipline and dependence on God through prayer and the study of God's Word for the wisdom in how to nurture my children in the admonition of the Lord. I will pursue this endeavor for a lifetime whether my children are in my home or not.

Finally, I believe that my end goal is not only for my children to walk in the Lord but this God-given vision would impact multiple generations to come, so help me God.

SMALL GROUP NOTES

Divide the large group into smaller groups of four to six people (depending on the number of facilitators available). Use the questions on pages 100-101 to review the homework from Lesson 5.

Recite the memory verse from Lesson 5:

> **Work out your own salvation with fear and trembling, for it is God who works in you, both to will and to work for his good pleasure. —Philippians 2:12b-13**

Use the material on pages 101-104 to discuss the main topics from this week's lesson.

The idea of unequally yoked describes a team of oxen where one was much bigger and stronger than the other with the result that they couldn't pull together as a team and plow a straight row. A believer and an unbeliever have difficulty pulling in one direction in marriage.

Recite this week's memory verse:

> *Therefore a man shall leave his father and his mother and hold fast to his wife, and they shall become one flesh.* —**Genesis 2:24**

Close the small-group discussion with a time of prayer.

Marriage — Part 1

Lesson 6

MARRIAGE
PART 1

LARGE GROUP SESSION

TWO PATHS

Here are the main themes we're concentrating on throughout this study (Two Paths):

- Every day we decide to either obey God or disobey. (Will we honor God or honor self?)
- There are consequences to each path—blessing or curse, heaven or hell.

REVIEW LESSON 5

Here are the main topics we covered during our last meeting:

- While God has given us a new heart and His Spirit, we have a responsibility too.
- We are to cooperate with God in growing in our Christian faith.
- To grow spiritually, we need to become men of the book, studying and applying the Bible to our lives. It is God's owner's manual for human beings.

- To grow spiritually, we have to talk to our heavenly Father. We do that through prayer.

- To grow spiritually, we need to be part of God's family, the local church.

KEY OBJECTIVES

Here are the key objectives for discussion this week:

- Identify the origin of marriage.

- Explore the problems sin caused for marriage.

- Understand the biblical reasons for marriage.

- Marriage is meant to be a lasting covenant.

MARRIAGE – PART 1

What do we learn about marriage from modern movies and TV shows?

What have you learned about marriage so far in your life?

As Christians, the first thing we need to understand about marriage is that the whole thing was God's idea.

> Then God said, "Let us make man in our image, after our likeness. And let them have dominion over the fish of the sea and over the birds of the heavens and over the livestock and over all the earth and over every creeping thing that creeps on the earth." So God created man in his own image, in the image of God he created him; male and female he created them. —**Genesis 1:26-27**

Men and women were created in God's image. God created them to rule over and care for His earthly creation, and to do it together.

Why is it important that God created human beings as male and female?

Men and women are different, each reflecting God's image in unique ways, each completing the other.

> Then the LORD God said, "It is not good that the man should be alone; I will make him a helper fit for him." And the rib that the Lord God had taken from the man he made into a woman and brought her to the man. Then the man said, "This at last is bone of my bones and flesh of my flesh; she shall be called Woman, because she was taken out of Man." Therefore a man shall leave his father and his mother and hold fast to his wife, and they shall become one flesh. And the man and his wife were both naked and were not ashamed.
> —**Genesis 2:18, 22-25**

What do these verses teach about the institution of marriage?

Why is it important that Adam and Eve were both naked and unashamed?

God designed marriage exactly the way He wanted it. Marriage is the core part of the family, and families are the building blocks of society. It's through marriage and family that we're supposed to learn the values of God's Kingdom and how to live as members of the church.

When Satan attacked Adam and Eve in the garden of Eden, he wasn't just attacking their relationship with God. He was also attacking their relationship with each other. And as a result of Adam and Eve's sin, marriage has been corrupted and damaged by sin. What was originally easy and natural, Adam leading out of love and humility and Eve following out of trust and submission, is now hard. Now it takes effort and work to overcome our selfishness.

One of the curses of the fall in Genesis 3:16 was that Eve's desire would be for her husband and that he would rule over her. The Hebrew word for *desire* means the desire for mastery or control. It is only used one other place in the Old Testament, when God warns Cain in Genesis 4:7 that sin is crouching at the door and its desire is for Cain. Sin wanted to control Cain. Because of the fall, Eve would desire mastery over her husband but he was to rule over her. Couples would now struggle to see who leads the marriage relationship. There would be conflict. Maybe you can relate to that idea. Again what was easy and natural became a struggle.

THE MALACHI DADS PLEDGE

As a Malachi Dad, I solemnly pledge to glorify God and build His Kingdom by prioritizing the raising of godly children, first in my family, then in the influencing of other men to do the same in theirs. I firmly believe that my transformed life in Christ—my life of integrity, pursuit of this vision, and the pursuit of godly character—will allow me to impact my children, family and others towards this end.

I will practice a life of daily discipline and dependence on God through prayer and the study of God's Word for the wisdom in how to nurture my children in the admonition of the Lord . I will pursue this endeavor for a lifetime whether my children are in my home or not.

Finally, I believe that my end goal is not only for my children to walk in the Lord but this God-given vision would impact multiple generations to come, so help me God.

What emotions do you experience when you read this pledge? Why?

Where can you find the wisdom and strength necessary to fulfill this pledge?

SMALL GROUP SESSION

REVIEW

What did you learn from this week's homework? What questions would you like to ask?

How has what you learned helped you understand God better?

How has what you learned helped you understand yourself better?

Recite the memory verse from Lesson 5:

> *Work out your own salvation with fear and trembling, for it is God who works in you, both to will and to work for His good pleasure.* —**Philippians 2:12b-13**

DISCUSSING MARRIAGE

One of the reasons God created marriage is because He knows that people need companionship and mutual support—it's not good for us to be alone (Genesis 2:18). That doesn't mean all people are supposed to be married, but marriage is one way we can find the community and encouragement we need.

How have you seen marriage provide encouragement and support to the people you know?

Raising children is another important purpose of marriage. God expects us to teach our children about Him and how to live as a disciple of Jesus.

> Train up a child in the way he should go; even when he is old he will not depart from it.
> **—Proverbs 22:6**

> Did He not make them one, with a portion of the Spirit in their union? And what was the one God seeking? Godly offspring. So guard yourselves in your spirit, and let none of you be faithless to the wife of your youth. **—Malachi 2:15**

What are some words you would use to describe your childhood?

What words would you use to describe your parents' marriage?

The Bible makes it clear that followers of Jesus should only choose to marry other Christians:

> Do not be unequally yoked with unbelievers. For what partnership has righteousness with lawlessness? Or what fellowship has light with darkness?
> **—2 Corinthians 6:14**

Why is it important for Christians to marry other Christians?

What advice would you give to a Christian who is married to an unbeliever?

God created the marriage covenant to be permanent, even if you are married to an unbeliever. He intended for a husband and wife to join together in unity for the rest of their lives, and He expected them never to violate that covenant.

Therefore a man shall leave his father and his mother and hold fast to his wife, and they shall become one flesh. —**Genesis 2:24**

Because the Lord was witness between you and the wife of your youth, to whom you have been faithless, though she is your companion and your wife by covenant. —**Malachi 2:14**

A wife is bound to her husband as long as he lives. But if her husband dies, she is free to be married to whom she wishes, only in the Lord. —**1 Corinthians 7:39**

How do these verses compare with our culture's view of marriage?

Sin has damaged the marriages within our society. One of the biggest ways marriages have been corrupted is through divorce.

What ideas or images come to mind when you hear the word divorce? Why?

And Pharisees came up to him and tested him by asking, "Is it lawful to divorce one's wife for any cause?" He answered, "Have you not read that he who created them from the beginning made them male and female, and said, 'Therefore a man shall leave his father and his mother and hold fast to his wife, and the two shall become one flesh'? So they are no longer two but one flesh. What therefore God has joined together, let not man separate." They said to him, "Why then did Moses command one to give a certificate of divorce and to send her away?" He said to them, "Because of your hardness of heart Moses

allowed you to divorce your wives, but from the
beginning it was not so. And I say to you: whoever
divorces his wife, except for sexual immorality,
and marries another, commits adultery."
—Matthew 19:3-9

Divorce was never part of God's plan for marriage. It is something that people have come up with because of sin and the choice to follow their own desires. Jesus tells us that marriage is one man and one woman in a one-flesh union for one lifetime.

How have you been impacted by divorce?

Where can you find hope in terms of recovering from your negative experiences?

As Christians, we need to understand that marriage is under attack today in several ways:

1. Our culture is attempting to change the definition of marriage away from what God intended. For example:

   • Marriage between a man and a man, or between a woman and a woman

   • Marriage between a group of people

   • Men and women choose to live together without getting married—they view marriage as unnecessary. People who lived together aren't married in God's eyes.

2. Our culture is also attempting to change the purpose of marriage away from what God desires.

   • People get married today for financial reasons.

   • People focus only on the sexual relationship, or choose to reject God's plan and engage in sex outside of marriage.

3. Our culture continues to push the idea that marriages can be ended for any reason through divorce.

Where do you see these attacks evident in modern society?

How have you experienced these attacks in your own life?

What are some practical steps you can take to make your experience with marriage more biblical?

REVIEW THE MALACHI DADS PLEDGE

THE MALACHI DADS PLEDGE

As a Malachi Dad, I solemnly pledge to glorify God and build His Kingdom by prioritizing the raising of godly children, first in my family, then in the influencing of other men to do the same in theirs. I firmly believe that my transformed life in Christ—my life of integrity, pursuit of this vision, and the pursuit of godly character—will allow me to impact my children, family, and others towards this end.

I will practice a life of daily discipline and dependence on God through prayer and the study of God's Word for the wisdom in how to nurture my children in the admonition of the Lord. I will pursue this endeavor for a lifetime whether my children are in my home or not.

Finally, I believe that my end goal is not only for my children to walk in the Lord but this God-given vision would impact multiple generations to come, so help me God.

SUMMARY:

• Marriage was designed by God.

• Marriage is for the mutual benefit of husbands and wives.

• Marriage is intended to be a lasting covenant.

Lesson 6

HOMEWORK

Complete the following assignments before the group gathers for Lesson 7.

Read Genesis 2:18-25, then answer the following questions:

1. How would you summarize the main idea of these verses?

2. What are three things God teaches us in this passage?

    a.

    b.

    c.

3. How can you apply these verses in your life?

Read Malachi 2:13-16, then answer the following questions:

1. How would you summarize the main idea of these verses?

2. God views marriage as a covenant, a sacred agreement between the man, the woman, and God. How does that impact your view of what marriage is and what marriage means?

3. How can you apply these verses in your life?

Review this week's memory verse:

> *Therefore a man shall leave his father and his mother and hold fast to his wife, and they shall become one flesh.* —**Genesis 2:24**

THE MALACHI DADS PLEDGE

As a Malachi Dad, I solemnly pledge to glorify God and build His Kingdom by prioritizing the raising of godly children, first in my family, then in the influencing of other men to do the same in theirs. I firmly believe that my transformed life in Christ—my life of integrity, pursuit of this vision, and the pursuit of godly character—will allow me to impact my children, family, and others towards this end.

I will practice a life of daily discipline and dependence on God through prayer and the study of God's Word for the wisdom in how to nurture my children in the admonition of the Lord. I will pursue this endeavor for a lifetime whether my children are in my home or not.

Finally, I believe that my end goal is not only for my children to walk in the Lord but this God-given vision would impact multiple generations to come, so help me God.

Marriage — Part 1

LESSON 7 **MEMORY VERSE**

*Husbands, love your wives, as Christ loved the
church and gave himself up for her.*

Ephesians 5:25

Lesson 7 : **Marriage — Part 2**
FACILITATOR NOTES

KEY TOPICS

• *Explore what it means to be a godly husband.*

• *Review the husband's role in a godly marriage.*

• *Discuss the role of sex in a healthy marriage relationship.*

LARGE GROUP NOTES

Begin with an opening prayer.

Be sure to mention that while society views marriage as a legal contract that can be easily broken, God views marriage as a lasting covenant between the man, the woman, and Himself. A covenant is much more binding than any contract because God is party to it.

Highlight Peter's warning that husbands who fail to live with their wives in an understanding way will not have their prayers answered by God. How we treat our wives affects our prayer lives.

Use the questions on pages 114–117 to begin addressing the topic of marriage according to God's Word.

The model for how a husband must love his wife is the way Christ loved the church and sacrificed Himself for her good and salvation. Self-sacrifice is the way we love our wives.

SMALL GROUP NOTES

Divide the large group into smaller groups of four to six people (depending on the number of facilitators available). Use the questions on page 118 to review the homework from Lesson 6. Then recite the memory verse from Lesson 6:

> Therefore a man shall leave his father and his
> mother and hold fast to his wife, and they shall
> become one flesh. **—Genesis 2:24**

Use the material on pages 118-120 to discuss the main topics from this week's lesson.

The point of the verse that speaks of sexual sin as transgressing and wronging a brother is the idea of defrauding or stealing. When a man gets involved in any kind of sexual sin, he is stealing something that doesn't belong to him—the love, affection, and intimacy that rightly belongs only to the husband of that woman. It would apply to premarital sex as well as adultery.

Recite this week's memory verse:

> Husbands, love your wives, as Christ loved the
> church and gave himself up for her. **—Ephesians
> 5:25**

Close the small-group discussion with a time of prayer.

Lesson 7

MARRIAGE
PART 2

LARGE GROUP SESSION

REVIEW LESSON 6

Here are the key topics we covered during our last meeting:

- Marriage was designed by God for the mutual benefit of husbands and wives.

- Sin brought conflict into marriage and caused damage in the family.

- Marriage is a lasting covenant in God's eyes.

- Marriage fulfills many purposes—companionship, support, raising godly children, and more.

- Marriage is under attack in our culture today.

KEY OBJECTIVES

Here are the objectives for discussion this week:

- Explore what it means to be a godly husband.

- Review the husband's role in a godly marriage.

- Discuss the role of sex in a healthy marriage relationship.

THE ROLE OF THE HUSBAND

Throughout your life, who taught you what it means to be a husband?

What did you learn most from those individuals?

As Christians, what we do in our families is vitally important. As husbands, we answer to God when it comes to the way we treat our wives and children.

> *But I want you to understand that the head of every man is Christ, the head of a wife is her husband, and the head of Christ is God.*
> **—1 Corinthians 11:3**

As the head of the home there are several responsibilities that God has asked of husbands. In this lesson we will look at just four of these responsibilities—they are leaders, providers, lovers of their wife, and life-long learners.

All husbands are leaders. God has called husbands to take a leadership role in their family, which includes supporting and sacrificing for their wife and children.

> *Wives, submit to your own husbands, as to the Lord. For the husband is the head of the wife even as Christ is the head of the church, his body, and is himself its Savior.* **—Ephesians 5:22-23**

> *Husbands, love your wives, as Christ loved the church and gave himself up for her.* **—Ephesians 5:25**

Do you consider yourself to be a leader? Explain.

What are some decisions that need to be made by the leader in a family?

How did Christ love the church?

Husbands are also called to be *providers*. We take care of our families, choosing to put their needs ahead of our own.

> *But if anyone does not provide for his relatives,*
> *and especially for members of his household,*
> *he has denied the faith and is worse than an*
> *unbeliever.* —**1 Timothy 5:8**

> *For even when we were with you, we would give*
> *you this command: If anyone is not willing to*
> *work, let him not eat. For we hear that some*
> *among you walk in idleness, not busy at work,*
> *but busybodies. Now such persons we command*
> *and encourage in the Lord Jesus Christ to do their*
> *work quietly and to earn their own living.*
> —**2 Thessalonians 3:10-12**

How do you respond to those verses? Why?

What steps can you take to improve as a provider for your family?

God doesn't want husbands to just lead his family and provide for his family, God also expects husbands to love their wives in a real and powerful way.

> *In the same way husbands should love their wives*
> *as their own bodies. He who loves his wife loves*
> *himself. For no one ever hated his own flesh, but*

nourishes and cherishes it, just as Christ does the church, because we are members of His body.
—Ephesians 5:28-30

Love is patient and kind; love does not envy or boast; it is not arrogant or rude. It does not insist on its own way; it is not irritable or resentful; it does not rejoice at wrongdoing, but rejoices with the truth. Love bears all things, believes all things, hopes all things, endures all things.
—1 Corinthians 13:4-7

Let your fountain be blessed, and rejoice in the wife of your youth, a lovely deer, a graceful doe. Let her breasts fill you at all times with delight; be intoxicated always in her love. **—Proverbs 5:18-19**

How do you respond to those verses?

When have you experienced the kind of love described in 1 Corinthians 13?

What are some ways that Christ showed love to the church?

How does sacrifice show love in a marriage relationship? How did Christ model that for husbands?

Love and bitterness don't mix, which is why husbands are called to use love as a way of solving conflict and strife in the family. Remember that anyone can take from other people, but true leaders (and true lovers) are the ones who choose to give.

Husbands are leaders, husbands are providers, husbands are lovers, and husbands are also learners. In order to love and lead your wife, you must *learn* who she is and what she needs. The more effort you make in learning about your wife the stronger your relationship will become. As you pursue her the more loved and valued she will feel. In your ongoing learning of your wife, you will show your love for her. She will feel loved and treasured by you, which will make it much easier for her to choose to follow your leadership.

> *Likewise, husbands, live with your wives in an understanding way, showing honor to the woman as the weaker vessel, since they are heirs with you of the grace of life, so that your prayers may not be hindered.* —**1 Peter 3:7**

What are some ways that a husband can learn about his wife?

Why is it a good thing in a marriage for the husband to constantly pursue his wife and try to learn more about her?

What steps can you take to be a better learner of your wife?

What happens if we fail to live with our wives in an understanding way?

In our time together we looked at some of the responsibilities that God expects from men who are married. When these roles of a husband are practiced and developed, they will build a stronger marriage relationship and honor God. In our small group discussion time, we will talk together about the role of sex within marriage. Sex is another important aspect in the marriage relationship that God has designed to build unity and intimacy, and foster a strong marriage.

SMALL GROUP SESSION

REVIEW

What did you learn from this week's homework? What questions would you like to ask?

How has what you learned helped you understand God better?

How has what you learned helped you understand yourself better?

Recite the memory verse from Lesson 6:

> *Therefore a man shall leave his father and his mother and hold fast to his wife, and they shall become one flesh.* —**Genesis 2:24**

DISCUSSION – MARRIAGE AND SEX

What does our culture teach us about sex?

What have you learned about sex from the church?

The first thing we need to understand about sex is that God created it as a gift to be enjoyed in the context of marriage. That was His plan for sex from the beginning.

> *Therefore a man shall leave his father and his mother and hold fast to his wife, and they shall become one flesh. And the man and his wife were both naked and were not ashamed.* —**Genesis 2:24-25**

> *Let marriage be held in honor among all, and let the marriage bed be undefiled, for God will judge the sexually immoral and adulterous.* —**Hebrews 13:4**

*But sexual immorality and all impurity or covet-
ousness must not even be named among you, as
is proper among saints.* —**Ephesians 5:3**

How do you respond to those verses? Why?

God's plan for sex is for a man and a woman to enjoy sex only
within the context of marriage.

*Let your fountain be blessed, and rejoice in the
wife of your youth, a lovely deer, a graceful doe.
Let her breasts fill you at all times with delight;
be intoxicated always in her love.* —**Proverbs
5:18-19**

How are we to view our sexual relationship in marriage?

Is it OK to enjoy sex with your wife?

*For this is the will of God, your sanctification: that
you abstain from sexual immorality; that each
one of you know how to control his own body in
holiness and honor, not in the passion of lust like
the Gentiles who do not know God; that no one
transgress and wrong his brother in this matter,
because the Lord is an avenger in all these
things, as we told you beforehand and solemnly
warned you.* —**1 Thessalonians 4:3-6**

Why is it sometimes so difficult for us to control our bodies?

How does sexual sin cheat and steal from others?

Why does God see this as wrong?

Sex isn't supposed to be a bullying point or a bargaining chip.
Instead, when two people are married, they should give themselves

to each other often, and they should give themselves as a gift. This kind of sexual intimacy pleases God.

> *But because of the temptation to sexual immorality, each man should have his own wife and each woman her own husband. The husband should give to his wife her conjugal rights, and likewise the wife to her husband. For the wife does not have authority over her own body, but the husband does. Likewise the husband does not have authority over his own body, but the wife does. Do not deprive one another, except perhaps by agreement for a limited time, that you may devote yourselves to prayer; but then come together again, so that Satan may not tempt you because of your lack of self-control.* —**1 Corinthians 7:2-5**

What do you know about God's view of sex in marriage now that you wish you knew when you were younger?

SUMMARY

In our lesson today, we talked about the roles of a godly husband. We discussed some of these responsibilities of a husband, highlighting that a husband needs to be a leader within the family. He needs to be a provider for his home and a lover to his wife. He is to pursue learning about his wife so he can meet the expectations God has set for being a godly husband. Lastly, in our small groups we talked about the important part that sex has within in the marriage relationship and how God views the role of sex in building a healthy marriage.

Lesson 7
HOMEWORK

Complete the following assignments before the group gathers for Lesson 8.

Read Ephesians 4:1-3, then answer the following questions.

1. How do these verses command Christians to behave? (What are we supposed to do?)

2. How do the commands in these verses apply to the roles of a husband?

3. In what ways can you improve at applying the commands in these verses?

Read these verses: Proverbs 10:12, 12:18, 13:10, 15:1, 16:21, 16:32, and 19:11. When you're finished, answer the following questions:

1. What are some common themes in these verses?

2. What are the benefits of wise speech?

3. What are the dangers of harsh speech?

4. How do these verses apply to your roles as a husband?

Review the verses you learned in the previous lessons.

Lesson 1:

> In the beginning, God created the heavens and the earth. —**Genesis 1:1**

Lesson 2:

> For all have sinned and fall short of the glory of God. —**Romans 3:23**

Lesson 3:

> For God so loved the world, that he gave his only Son, that whoever believes in him should not perish but have eternal life. —**John 3:16**

Lesson 4:

> And I will give you a new heart, and a new spirit I will put within you. And I will remove the heart of stone from your flesh and give you a heart of flesh. —**Ezekiel 36:26**

Lesson 5:

> Work out your own salvation with fear and trembling, for it is God who works in you, both to will and to work for his good pleasure. —**Philippians 2:12b-13**

Lesson 6:

> Therefore a man shall leave his father and his mother and hold fast to his wife, and they shall become one flesh. —**Genesis 2:24**

Review this week's memory verse:

> Husbands, love your wives, as Christ loved the church and gave himself up for her.
> —**Ephesians 5:25**

LESSON 8 **MEMORY VERSE**

*In the fear of the Lord one has strong confidence,
and his children will have a refuge.*

Proverbs 14:26

Lesson 8 : **Fathering — Part 1**
FACILITATOR NOTES

KEY TOPICS

• *Clarify the relationship between fathers and children.*

• *Identify the characteristics of a godly family environment.*

• *Explore a warning to fathers.*

LARGE GROUP NOTES

Begin with an opening prayer. Review the Malachi Dads Pledge. Use the questions on pages 128-129 to begin addressing the topic of fathering according to God's Word.

A strong marriage is required to be a good parent. The better we love our wives, the more secure our children will feel. Our first commitment must be to our wives.

Our children are given to us as a blessing, not a burden. Be sure to emphasize the need for us to be grateful for our children and to let our kids know how glad we are to be their fathers.

The idea of children as arrows in the hand of the warrior is meant to communicate that even as arrows allow a warrior to defend himself in battle, children also help defend the father as he grows older from physical attack or from accusations in court of the elders at the city gates. This is to help explain Psalm 127:3-4.

SMALL GROUP NOTES

Divide the large group into smaller groups of four to six people (depending on the number of facilitators available). Use the questions on page 130 to review the homework from Lesson 7.

Recite the memory verse from Lesson 7:

> *Husbands, love your wives, as Christ loved*
> *the church and gave himself up for her.*
> **—Ephesians 5:25**

Discuss the main topics of this week's lesson using the material on pages 130-134. Emphasize that fear of the Lord and maintaining a strong relationship with God is also critical to be an effective father.

Recite this week's memory verse:

> *In the fear of the Lord one has strong confidence,*
> *and his children will have a refuge.* **—Proverbs**
> **14:26**

Close the small-group discussion with a time of prayer.

Lesson 8

FATHERING
PART 1

LARGE GROUP SESSION

KEY BELIEFS

Remember the key beliefs for this study:

- God is real, and He is in charge of all things.

- God's Word is true. God gave us the Bible for our benefit and guidance. It is our owner's manual.

- The Bible is all we need to understand our world, and to live in a way that pleases God. Following the Bible allows us to help our families, neighbors, and country.

- We will choose one of two paths: we will either obey and honor God or disobey and honor ourselves. Each path has consequences.

REVIEW LESSON 7

Here are the key topics we covered during our last meeting:

- A husband is a leader, provider, lover, and learner.

- Husbands are accountable to God for the way they treat their family.

- Marriage between a man and a woman is the only place for sex.

- Sex is a gift from God designed to be enjoyed, but not abused.

KEY OBJECTIVES

Here are the key objectives for discussion this week:

- Clarify the relationship between fathers and children.

- Identify the characteristics of a godly family environment.

- Explore a warning to fathers.

FATHERING – PART 1

What's the most important relationship within a family? Explain.

> He [Jesus] answered, "Have you not read that He who created them from the beginning made them male and female, and said, 'Therefore a man shall leave his father and his mother and hold fast to his wife, and the two shall become one flesh'? So they are no longer two but one flesh. What therefore God has joined together, let not man separate." —**Matthew 19:4-6**

> When a man is newly married, he shall not go out with the army or be liable for any other public duty. He shall be free at home one year to be happy with his wife whom he has taken.
> —**Deuteronomy 24:5**

The primary relationship in the family is the relationship between husband and wife. The husband-wife relationship is designed to be permanent. Children should leave their parents to start their own homes and families. The bond between a husband and wife even takes priority over national defense!

What do movies and TV shows teach about the relationship between husband and wife?

Unfortunately, our culture has the family priority reversed. Children are given priority over the parents in most families today; the activities and schedule revolve around the children, not the parents. As a result, parents become worn out and kids become self-centered and slow to mature.

What does culture teach about the relationships between parents and kids?

When we keep the proper priorities in our homes, we can fully appreciate that children are a blessing given to us by God.

Children bring us joy, but they also represent a responsibility. Parents are stewards charged to raise their children in a way that helps them worship and honor God from their youngest days.

> *Behold, children are a heritage from the Lord,*
> *the fruit of the womb a reward. Like arrows in the*
> *hand of a warrior are the children of one's youth.*
> **—Psalm 127:3-4**

> *Did he not make them one, with a portion of the*
> *Spirit in their union? And what was the one God*
> *seeking? Godly offspring. So guard yourselves in*
> *your spirit, and let none of you be faithless to the*
> *wife of your youth.* **—Malachi 2:15**

SUMMARY:

- It is God who gives children to us.

- Parents are responsible to raise their children in a godly manner.

- Parenting is both an honor and a responsibility, both of which are given by God.

SMALL GROUP SESSION

REVIEW

What did you learn from this week's homework? What questions would you like to ask?

How has what you learned helped you understand God better?

How has what you learned helped you understand yourself better?

Recite the memory verse from Lesson 7:

> Husbands, love your wives, as Christ loved the church and gave himself up for her. —**Ephesians 5:25**

DISCUSSING FATHERING

What ideas or images come to mind when you hear the word fear? Why?

The Bible teaches about several characteristics godly fathers should have, but the fear of the Lord is one of the most important characteristics fathers must have.

Blessed is everyone who fears the Lord, who walks in his ways! You shall eat the fruit of the labor of your hands; you shall be blessed, and it shall be well with you. Your wife will be like a fruitful vine within your house; your children will be like olive shoots around your table. Behold, thus shall the man be blessed who fears the Lord.
—**Psalm 128:1-4**

What do these verses teach about healthy families?

How would you define what it means to fear the Lord as a father?

The fear of the Lord is a reverent awe of God that leads to a desire to obey, trust, and honor Him. This attitude is a gift of the Lord and leads to many blessings in our lives.

Let's look at some other characteristics of godly families. First, the home should be a place where all people feel respected—including Mom and Dad.

Honor your father and your mother, as the Lord your God commanded you, that your days may be long, and that it may go well with you in the land that the Lord your God is giving you.
—**Deuteronomy 5:16**

If one curses his father or his mother, his lamp will be put out in utter darkness. —**Proverbs 20:20**

Was your home a place of respect when you were a child? Explain.

As parents, how can we know when our children respect us?

How can we help our children respect us?

Second, a godly home should be a place of safety and refuge. Fear, anger, and unforgiveness have no place in the home. Instead, all family members should look forward to being home. As fathers, we have a great opportunity to influence our home environments.

> In the fear of the Lord one has strong confidence, and his children will have a refuge. —**Proverbs 14:26**

> Children, obey your parents in the Lord, for this is right. "Honor your father and mother" (this is the first commandment with a promise), "that it may go well with you and that you may live long in the land." Fathers, do not provoke your children to anger, but bring them up in the discipline and instruction of the Lord. —**Ephesians 6:1-4**

What does it look like when family members don't feel safe within their homes? What happens in those situations?

What steps can we take as fathers to make sure our homes are places of safety and refuge?

Third, godly homes are places where people learn about God and learn how to experience His presence. They are places where children receive moral training and parents choose to do what is right. This is one of our main responsibilities as fathers.

> And these words that I command you today shall be on your heart. You shall teach them diligently to your children, and shall talk of them when you sit in your house, and when you walk by the way, and when you lie down, and when you rise. You

*shall bind them as a sign on your hand, and they
shall be as frontlets between your eyes. You shall
write them on the doorposts of your house and on
your gates.* —**Deuteronomy 6:6-9**

What must fathers do before they can diligently teach their children the word?

What are the different types of opportunities described in these verses?

What do these opportunities look like in our lives today?

> *My son, keep your father's commandment, and
> forsake not your mother's teaching. Bind them
> on your heart always; tie them around your neck.
> When you walk, they will lead you; when you lie
> down, they will watch over you; and when you
> awake, they will talk with you.* —**Proverbs
> 6:20-23**

How can you teach your children about God in your current situation?

One of the worst things we can do as fathers (and husbands) is to lash out in anger. Instead of lashing out in anger, fathers need to provide guidelines for their children to help them understand what God desires for them.

> *Husbands, love your wives, and do not be harsh
> with them. Children, obey your parents in every-
> thing, for this pleases the Lord. Fathers, do not
> provoke your children, lest they become discour-
> aged.* —**Colossians 3:19-21**

Know this, my beloved brothers: let every person be quick to hear, slow to speak, slow to anger; for the anger of man does not produce the righteousness of God. —**James 1:19-20**

How would you describe your experiences with discipline as a child?

How do we discipline our children without lashing out in anger?

REVIEW THE MALACHI DADS PLEDGE

THE MALACHI DADS PLEDGE

As a Malachi Dad, I solemnly pledge to glorify God and build His Kingdom by prioritizing the raising of godly children, first in my family, then in the influencing of other men to do the same in theirs. I firmly believe that my transformed life in Christ—my life of integrity, pursuit of this vision, and the pursuit of godly character—will allow me to impact my children, family, and others towards this end.

I will practice a life of daily discipline and dependence on God through prayer and the study of God's Word for the wisdom in how to nurture my children in the admonition of the Lord. I will pursue this endeavor for a lifetime whether my children are in my home or not.

Finally, I believe that my end goal is not only for my children to walk in the Lord but this God-given vision would impact multiple generations to come, so help me God.

SUMMARY:

- The relationship between husband and wife is primary in a family.

- A godly father must fear the Lord.

- Families should be a place of respect, honor, safety and godly teaching.

- Fathers are warned not to lash out in anger and provoke their children.

Lesson 8

HOMEWORK

Complete the following assignments before the group gathers for Lesson 9.

Make a list of everything you appreciate about each of your children. Be as specific as you can.

Is there any person in your family with whom you have difficulty communicating? Who?

1. What can you do to remove barriers?

2. What can you do to improve communication?

What are some ways you have provoked your children or lashed out in anger?

What steps can you take in the coming weeks to guide your children in a godly way?

Review this week's memory verse:

> *In the fear of the Lord one has strong confidence, and his children will have a refuge.* —**Proverbs 14:26**

THE MALACHI DADS PLEDGE

As a Malachi Dad, I solemnly pledge to glorify God and build His Kingdom by prioritizing the raising of godly children, first in my family, then in the influencing of other men to do the same in theirs. I firmly believe that my transformed life in Christ—my life of integrity, pursuit of this vision, and the pursuit of godly character—will allow me to impact my children, family, and others towards this end.

I will practice a life of daily discipline and dependence on God through prayer and the study of God's Word for the wisdom in how to nurture my children in the admonition of the Lord. I will pursue this endeavor for a lifetime whether my children are in my home or not.

Finally, I believe that my end goal is not only for my children to walk in the Lord but this God-given vision would impact multiple generations to come, so help me God.

LESSON 9 **MEMORY VERSE**

Train up a child in the way he should go;
even when he is old he will not depart from it.

Proverbs 22:6

Lesson 9 : **Fathering — Part 2**
FACILITATOR NOTES

KEY TOPICS

• *Define godly discipline.*

• *Consider how to apply godly discipline.*

• *Identify culturally unbiblical ways to raise children.*

• *Summarize biblical advice for stepfamilies.*

LARGE GROUP NOTES

Begin with an opening prayer. Review the Malachi Dads Pledge.

The key idea in Proverbs 22:6 about training up a child in the way he should go is about finding each child's bent and then helping channel them in that direction. We need to be careful about forcing children to be what we want them to be rather than who God created them to be. Fathers should encourage their children in their strengths.

Use the questions on pages 142-144 to continue exploring what it means to be a godly father.

SMALL GROUP NOTES

Divide the large group into smaller groups of four to six people (depending on the number of facilitators available). Use the questions on page 145 to review the homework from Lesson 8.

Recite the memory verse from Lesson 8:

> *In the fear of the Lord one has strong confidence,*

and his children will have a refuge. —**Proverbs 14:26**

Discuss the main topics of this week's lesson using the material on pages 145-149. Remember that the most effective tool we have as fathers is a consistent example. How we live gives power to our parenting or undermines it.

Recite this week's memory verse:

> Train up a child in the way he should go; even when he is old he will not depart from it.
> —**Proverbs 22:6**

Close the small-group discussion with a time of prayer.

Lesson 9

FATHERING
PART 2

LARGE GROUP SESSION

Remember our Two Paths theme for this study:

- Every day we decide to either obey God or disobey Him—to honor God or to honor ourselves.

- There are consequences to each path.

REVIEW LESSON 8

Here are the key topics we covered during our last meeting:

- Marriage is the primary human relationship—the connection between husband and wife.

- A godly husband and father must fear the Lord.

- A godly family environment is a place of respect, safety and teaching.

- Fathers should not provoke their children or lash out in anger.

KEY OBJECTIVES

Here are the key objectives for discussion this week:

- Define godly discipline.

- Consider how to apply godly discipline.

- Identify culturally unbiblical ways to raise children.

- Summarize biblical advice for stepfamilies.

FATHERING – PART 2

What does our culture teach us about the relationship between fathers and their children?

We need to understand that God intended fathers to be one of the most significant relationships and influences in the lives of children, and He created children to naturally look up to their fathers. Children want to be proud of their dads and have to be convinced otherwise.

> *Grandchildren are the crown of the aged, and the glory of children is their fathers.* —**Proverbs 17:6**

Discipline is a natural part of the relationship between fathers and children. Even though they don't know it or appreciate it, godly discipline is one of the things kids need most from their dads.

The word *discipline* is often used negatively. Actually, discipline is meant to be a loving approach to teaching children appropriate behavior. It comes from the word disciple and literally means "to teach" or "to mold." Children need discipline to become healthy, mature adults.

My son, do not regard lightly the discipline of the Lord, nor be weary when reproved by Him. For the Lord disciplines the one He loves, and chastises every son whom He receives. It is for discipline that you have to endure. God is treating you as sons. For what son is there whom his father does not discipline? If you are left without discipline, in which all have participated, then you are illegitimate children and not sons. Besides this, we have had earthly fathers who disciplined us and we respected them. Shall we not much more be subject to the Father of spirits and live?
—Hebrews 12:5b-9

How would you summarize the main message of these verses?

Where have you seen godly discipline done well?

Train up a child in the way he should go; even when he is old he will not depart from it.
—Proverbs 22:6

What's your first reaction to this verse? Why?

Let's spend a few minutes reviewing some biblical tips for godly parenting:

- Children left to themselves will go in the wrong direction (Proverbs 29:15). Free range parenting rarely works.

- If you allow children to go their own way, they will likely do so their whole life.

  -- Proverbs 22:6 is advice, not a promise.

  -- Even good parents can have bad children.

- Never discipline a child in uncontrolled anger, because wrath does not produce righteousness (James 1:19-20).

- Discipline with the goal of raising a child who is wise.

- Discipline is for changing behavior, not punishment—the goal is to develop godly habits.

What questions do you have about these biblical tips?

What other tips or themes from the Bible can help us discipline children in a godly way?

Let's finish this portion of the study by reviewing some practical tips for godly parenting:

- Never discipline in public. Kids will focus on the people watching, not the issue being corrected.

- Discipline children because they did wrong, not because they made you angry or embarrassed. (Be sure to hug and pray afterwards.)

- During and after discipline, be sure to explain what was wrong according to God's rules.

What questions do you have about these practical tips?

What other tips or ideas can help us discipline children in a godly way?

SMALL GROUP

REVIEW

What did you learn from this week's homework? What questions would you like to ask?

How has what you learned helped you understand God better?

How has what you learned helped you understand yourself better?

Recite the memory verse from Lesson 8:

> In the fear of the Lord one has strong confidence,
> and his children will have a refuge. —**Proverbs
> 14:26**

DISCUSSING FATHERING

What do you remember most fondly about your father growing up?

Looking back, in what areas did your father struggle as a parent?

Godly fathers are committed to disciplining their children.

> And have you forgotten the exhortation that
> addresses you as sons? "My son, do not regard
> lightly the discipline of the Lord, nor be weary
> when reproved by him. For the Lord disciplines
> the one he loves, and chastises every son whom
> he receives." —**Hebrews 12:5-6**

In the same way God, our heavenly Father, disciplines us for our good, fathers must discipline their kids for their good.

How should the age of our children influence the decisions we make about discipline?

One type of discipline is reproof. This is any kind of verbal discipline, including instruction, encouragement, correction, warning, teaching, prayer, persuasion, and more.

> *All Scripture is breathed out by God and profitable for teaching, for reproof, for correction, and for training in righteousness, that the man of God may be complete, equipped for every good work.*
> —**2 Timothy 3:16-17**

> *Whoever loves discipline loves knowledge, but he who hates reproof is stupid.* —**Proverbs 12:1**

How do you respond to these verses?

What are some godly ways to reprove our children?

What are some other ways we can discipline our children according to 2 Timothy 3:16-17?

What is the goal of using God's Word to discipline our children?

How does our culture teach parents to discipline their children?

Let's look at some more tips in the Bible for how to discipline children in a godly way. First, as we saw last week, we should remember that anger doesn't help us achieve godly goals as fathers.

> *A soft answer turns away wrath, but a harsh word stirs up anger. The tongue of the wise commends knowledge, but the mouths of fools pour out folly.*
> —**Proverbs 15:1-2**

Second, we can help our cause as fathers by teaching our children about God, and by reminding our children of how God has blessed our families in the past.

> *And he said to the people of Israel, "When your children ask their fathers in times to come, 'What do these stones mean?' then you shall let your children know, 'Israel passed over this Jordan on dry ground.' For the Lord your God dried up the waters of the Jordan for you until you passed over, as the Lord your God did to the Red Sea, which he dried up for us until we passed over, so that all the peoples of the earth may know that the hand of the Lord is mighty, that you may fear the Lord your God forever."* —**Joshua 4:21-24**

> *Hear this, you elders; give ear, all inhabitants of the land! Has such a thing happened in your days, or in the days of your fathers? Tell your children of it, and let your children tell their children, and their children to another generation.* —**Joel 1:2-3**

When have you been successful at teaching your children about God?

What are some of the best things God has done for your family?

Fathers need to be careful not to practice double standards (say one thing, but do another). Also, both parents need to be in agreement in disciplining their children. There must be a united front.

Ensure that all teaching and admonition is clear to the child—that he or she understands. Be sure your teaching is biblical and that you clearly understand why you believe it. Children will pick up on your doubt if it's there.

Another key to godly fathering is establishing house rules that are based on the truths found in God's Word.

> Let the word of Christ dwell in you richly, teaching and admonishing one another in all wisdom, singing psalms and hymns and spiritual songs, with thankfulness in your hearts to God.
> —**Colossians 3:16**

> And let us consider how to stir up one another to love and good works. —**Hebrews 10:24**

How does your family determine house rules?

How can you make sure your family's rules are based on God's Word?

DISCUSSING MENTORING

Another element of disciplining our children is mentoring.

A mentor is someone who:
- Listens well.
- Acts as a positive role model.
- Seeks teachable moments.
- Provides guidance and advice.
- Offers encouragement and support.

What are some ways you can mentor your children?

IMPORTANT TIPS FOR STEP FAMILIES

With many people being in blended families today, step parenting is important. Consider the following guideline:

- To have a successful step family, you must keep a high view of marriage—the relationship between husband and wife takes priority over children.

- A child-centered home will always experience trouble because the children will eventually grow up and leave—this leaves you as a couple with a relationship in shambles.

- Your commitment to any of your children is temporary; your commitment to your spouse is for a lifetime.

- For children, your example of setting your spouse ahead of them is the model they need to see for their own future marriage (Ephesians 5:22-33).

- The powerful and natural desire to love your own children must be surrendered to the higher priority of being a godly mate and loving spouse.

- The one thing you must insist upon, whether they are your children, her children or both your children, is that they must treat your wife with respect. Your job is to respect and protect her.

- Be responsible for your current family! Own your personal responsibility, regardless of bad behavior by others.

- Remember, the battle is in the heart and the mind in your children.

Lesson 9

HOMEWORK

Complete the following assignments before the group gathers for Lesson 10.

Read Ephesians 4:29, then answer the following questions:

1. What three things should we consider before speaking?

2. How can this help you discipline your children?

3. How can you apply this verse to your life?

Look again at Ephesians 6:1-4, then answer the following questions:

1. What are the truths expressed in these verses?

2. What are the challenges and commands expressed in these verses?

3. How do these verses connect with Ephesians 4:29?

Review this week's memory verse:

> *Train up a child in the way he should go; even when he is old he will not depart from it.*
> **—Proverbs 22:6**

LESSON 10 **MEMORY VERSE**

Your word is a lamp for my feet,
a light on my path.

Psalm 119:105

Lesson 10 : **Fathering** — **Part 3**
FACILITATOR NOTES

KEY TOPICS

• *Define the general objective for godly training: to love God and love people.*

• *Learn how to use the Bible to teach children about sex.*

• *Read suggested verses for pride, drinking, honesty, money, and anger.*

LARGE GROUP NOTES

Begin with an opening prayer. Use the questions on pages 156–158 to continue exploring what it means to be a godly father.

The key point to make during your time teaching in the large group portion of this lesson is that as a father you are tasked by God to model how to love God and love others. When your children see this modeled and then taught daily, they will more easily practice that same lifestyle that you set before them.

SMALL GROUP NOTES

Divide the large group into smaller groups of four to six people (depending on the number of facilitators available). Use the questions on page 158 to review the homework from Lesson 9.

Recite the memory verse from Lesson 9:

> *Train up a child in the way he should go; even when he is old he will not depart from it.*
> —**Proverbs 22:6**

Discuss the main topics of this week's lesson using the material on pages 158-161.

It can be tough to teach your children about the consequences of sexual sin, particularly if this has been a struggle personally. You don't want to come across hypocritically. Encourage your group to be as open and honest with past failures and the lessons that have been learned. Sometimes your most powerful teaching moments come from lessons learned from failure. Be sure to strengthen your teaching in this area by living a God-honoring example before your children.

Be sure to work through the important topics that are listed at the end of your small group section. Have each member of the small group read and share at least one verse.

Make a challenge in the group for how they will practice at least one of these topics during the week so that they can better instruct their children by setting an example.

Recite this week's memory verse:

> Your word is a lamp for my feet, a light on my path. —**Psalm 119:105**

Close the small-group discussion with a time of prayer.

Lesson 10

FATHERING
PART 3

LARGE GROUP SESSION

REVIEW LESSON 9

Remember the main purpose of our study: to provide an overview of what the Bible says about God, man, marriage, and fathering.

Here are the key topics we covered during our last meeting:

- Children look up to their fathers.

- Children need discipline; their hearts are foolish when young.

- Godly families (including stepfamilies) have a high view of marriage where the relationship between husband and wife is the priority.

KEY OBJECTIVES

Here are the key objectives for discussion this week:

- Define the general objective for godly training: to love God and love people.

- Learn how to use the Bible to teach children about sex.

- Read suggested verses for pride, drinking, honesty, money, and anger.

FATHERING – PART 3

What would you say is the most significant thing you can teach your child?

> *And one of them, a lawyer, asked him a question to test him. "Teacher, which is the great commandment in the Law?" And he said to him, "You shall love the Lord your God with all your heart and with all your soul and with all your mind. This is the great and first commandment. And a second is like it: You shall love your neighbor as yourself. On these two commandments depend all the Law and the Prophets."* —**Matthew 22:35-40**

These verses help us understand our main goal as fathers. We teach and discipline our kids in order to help them love God and others.

Why is this an important goal for us as fathers?

If we love God, we will obey Him. If we love other people, we will treat them like we want to be treated. This is what we hope to accomplish in the lives of our children. This is best done through your faithful obedience to God. Your children need to see you, as their father, loving God and loving other people.

Remember it is NOT "Do as I say, not as I do"! Hypocrisy has no place in training your children to be followers of Jesus Christ.

Another important goal for fathering and godly discipline is to help our children realize that we all follow one of two paths. We either obey God each day or we disobey Him—and each path has consequences.

Blessed is the man who walks not in the counsel of the wicked, nor stands in the way of sinners, nor sits in the seat of scoffers; but his delight is in the law of the Lord, and on his law he meditates day and night. He is like a tree planted by streams of water that yields its fruit in its season, and its leaf does not wither. In all that he does, he prospers. The wicked are not so, but are like chaff that the wind drives away. Therefore the wicked will not stand in the judgment, nor sinners in the congregation of the righteous; for the Lord knows the way of the righteous, but the way of the wicked will perish. —**Psalm 1:1-6**

What do you like best about these verses? Why?

How do these verses help us understand the idea of two paths?

Finally, it's important for us to use godly discipline as parents because it helps our children understand the seriousness of sin—and that sin always brings consequences.

But each person is tempted when he is lured and enticed by his own desire. Then desire when it has conceived gives birth to sin, and sin when it is fully grown brings forth death. —**James 1:14-15**

The end of the matter; all has been heard. Fear God and keep his commandments, for this is the whole duty of man. For God will bring every deed into judgment, with every secret thing, whether good or evil. —**Ecclesiastes 12:13-14**

Why is it important for everyone to understand the seriousness of sin?

How can we teach our children about the consequences of sin?

> But what comes out of the mouth proceeds from the heart, and this defiles a person. For out of the heart come evil thoughts, murder, adultery, sexual immorality, theft, false witness, slander. These are what defile a person. —**Matthew 15:18-20a**

What do these verses teach about the source of sin in all of us?

SMALL GROUP SESSION

REVIEW

What did you learn from this week's homework? What questions would you like to ask?

How has what you learned helped you understand God better?

How has what you learned helped you understand yourself better?

Recite the memory verse from Lesson 9:

> Train up a child in the way he should go; even when he is old he will not depart from it.
> —**Proverbs 22:6**

DISCUSSING FATHERING

How would you summarize the main goals for fathering and godly discipline?

What emotions do you experience when you think about those goals? Why?

As parents, we don't have all the wisdom we need to teach our children about the bigger questions of life. Thankfully, we can rely on God's Word when it comes time for us to guide our children down the more complicated roads of life.

For example, the Bible helps us teach our children about sex in two main ways. First, we can help our children understand God's plan for sex and sexuality.

> *Therefore a man shall leave his father and his mother and hold fast to his wife, and they shall become one flesh. And the man and his wife were both naked and were not ashamed.*
> **—Genesis 2:24-25**

> *Let marriage be held in honor among all, and let the marriage bed be undefiled, for God will judge the sexually immoral and adulterous.*—**Hebrews 13:4**

How would you summarize God's plan for sex and sexuality?

Second, the Bible helps us understand the consequences of rebelling against God's plan for sex.

> *He who commits adultery lacks sense; he who does it destroys himself. He will get wounds and dishonor, and his disgrace will not be wiped away.*
> `**Proverbs 6:32-33**

> *Flee from sexual immorality. Every other sin a person commits is outside the body, but the sexu-*

ally immoral person sins against his own body. Or do you not know that your body is a temple of the Holy Spirit within you, whom you have from God? You are not your own, for you were bought with a price. So glorify God in your body.
—1 Corinthians 6:18-20

What are some of the consequences we receive when we go against God's plan for sex and sexuality?

How can you teach these consequences to your children?

The Bible also helps us teach about sex and consequences because it tells the story of several men and women who encountered God's plan in different ways. For example:

- Joseph's encounter with Potiphar's wife helps us understand how to deal with sexual temptation (Genesis 39:6-23).
- David's encounter with Bathsheba offers a negative example for dealing with temptation (2 Samuel 11:2-17).
- Psalm 51 is a great example of David's sorrow after giving in to temptation and committing sexual sin.

The Bible also helps us understand (and teach our children) how to avoid sin.

I have made a covenant with my eyes; how then could I gaze at a virgin? What would be my portion from God above and my heritage from the Almighty on high? Is not calamity for the unrighteous, and disaster for the workers of iniquity? Does not he see my ways and number all my steps? **—Job 31:1-4**

*How can a young man keep his way pure? By
guarding it according to your word. With my
whole heart I seek you; let me not wander from
your commandments! I have stored up your word
in my heart*, that I might not sin against you.
—**Psalm 119:9-11**

What do these verses teach about avoiding sin?

OTHER KEY TOPICS

The Bible helps us teach and correct our children on several
important topics. The Bible also reminds us that we as fathers need
to apply these verses to our own lives and set the right example
for our children. Here are some examples with suggested Scripture
readings:

- **To teach about pride:** Proverbs 8:13, 11:2, 16:18, 18:12,
21:24, 27:1, 29:23; Daniel 4:4-37; 2 Samuel 24:1-25

- **To teach about drinking:** Proverbs 20:1, 23:19-21, 23:29-35; 1
Corinthians 5:11, 6:9-11; 1 Peter 4:1-4

- **To teach about honesty:** Exodus 20:16; Psalm 19:14; Proverbs
8:6-8, 12:22, 19:9; Ephesians 4:15, 4:25, 4:29

- **To teach about money:** Matthew 6:24; Romans 13:8; 1 Timothy
6:10

- **To teach about anger:** Proverbs 10:12, 12:16, 14:16-17,
15:1, 15:18, 19:11, 25:28, 29:22, 30:33; Matthew 5:21-22;
Ephesians 4:26; Colossians 3:8; James 1:19-20

Lesson 10

HOMEWORK

Complete the following assignments before the group gathers for Lesson 11.

Read Daniel 4:4-37, then answer the following questions:

1. What's your initial reaction to these verses? Why?

2. How can you use these verses to teach children about pride?

3. What's the difference between healthy pride and sinful pride?

4. What are some ways to prevent sinful pride?

Read Exodus 20:1-20, then answer the following questions:

1. Which of these commandments did you struggle with as a child?

2. Which do you struggle with now?

3. How can you teach these commandments to your children?

Review this week's memory verse:

> Your word is a lamp for my feet, a light on my path. —**Psalm 119:105**

LESSON 11 **MEMORY VERSE**

*And he will turn the hearts of
fathers to their children and the hearts
of children to their fathers.*

Malachi 4:6

Lesson 11 : **Inmate Challenge**
FACILITATOR NOTES

KEY TOPICS

• *Explore what it means to live as a godly man while incarcerated.*

• *Explore what it looks like to be a godly spouse while in prison.*

• *Explore how to love and discipline children while incarcerated.*

LARGE GROUP NOTES

Begin with an opening prayer. Review the Malachi Dads Pledge.

Make sure you preview the video and read the questions ahead of time. For the large-group portion of this gathering, show the video portion of the Inmate Challenge DVD, produced by Lifeline Global Ministries™.

This video is an unscripted, unedited response to this simple question: "If you could talk to other inmates across the country about being a godly man, a godly spouse, and a godly parent, what would you say?"

Ask: As you listen to the stories and the wisdom of the inmates featured in this video, use the questions on page 170 as a way of recording your reactions to what you see.

REACTIONS

Allow participants to record their personal reactions as they watch the video.

TEACHING CONTENT

Allow participants to record some of the main principles taught by Ron, Darryl, and George.

Ask: What have you learned about being a father?

Ask: What have you learned about being a provider for your family?

Ask: What have you learned about good and bad habits?

Ask: What have you learned about being a godly member of your extended family?

MORE ABOUT LIFELINE GLOBAL MINISTRIES™

Since 2004, Awana Lifeline (now Lifeline Global Ministries™) has been working with prisons around the country to help inmate fathers understand and live out their responsibilities as fathers, despite being incarcerated.

Launched at Louisiana State Penitentiary at Angola, our work has now reached several dozen other prisons across the country, all with the goal of reaching our mission: to help men build a legacy of faith in Christ among their families.

SMALL GROUP NOTES

Divide the large group into smaller groups of four to six people (depending on the number of facilitators available). Use the questions on page 171 to review the homework from Lesson 10.

Recite the memory verse from Lesson 10:

> Your word is a lamp for my feet, a light on my path. —**Psalm 119:105**

Discuss the main topics of this week's lesson using the material on pages 171-174.

Recite this week's memory verse:

> And he will turn the hearts of fathers to their children and the hearts of children to their fathers. —**Malachi 4:6**

Close the small-group discussion with a time of prayer.

Inmate Challenge

Lesson 11

INMATE CHALLENGE

LARGE GROUP SESSION

REVIEW LESSON 10

Here are the key topics we covered during our last meeting:

- Highlight the basic goal of godly training: to love God and love people.

- How to use the Bible to teach children about sex and other issues.

KEY OBJECTIVES

Here are the key objectives for discussion this week:

- Explore what it means to live as a godly man while incarcerated.

- Explore what it looks like to be a godly spouse while in prison.

- Explore how to love and discipline children while incarcerated.

INMATE CHALLENGE

Watch the video from the Inmate Challenge DVD, produced by Lifeline Global Ministries™.

This video is an unscripted, unedited response to this simple question: "If you could talk to other inmates across the country about being a godly man, a godly spouse, and a godly parent, what would you say?"

As you listen to the stories and the wisdom of the inmates featured in this video, use the following questions as a way of recording your reactions to what you see.

REACTIONS TO THE VIDEO

Record your personal reactions as you watch the video.

What did you like best about the conversation between Ron, Darryl, and George?

How is God speaking to you through their words?

Which of their ideas or suggestions can you apply in your life?

TEACHING CONTENT

Record some of the main principles taught by Ron, Darryl, and George.

What have you learned about being a father?

What have you learned about being a provider for your family?

What have you learned about good and bad habits?

What have you learned about being a godly member of your extended family?

MORE ABOUT LIFELINE GLOBAL MINISTRIES

Since 2004, Awana Lifeline (now Lifeline Global Ministries™) has been working with prisons around the country to help inmate fathers understand and live out their responsibilities as fathers, despite being incarcerated.

Launched at Louisiana state Penitentiary at Angola, our work has now reached several dozen other prisons across the country, all with the goal of reaching our mission: to help men build a legacy of faith in Christ among their families.

SMALL GROUP SESSION

REVIEW

What did you learn from this week's homework? What questions would you like to ask?

How has what you learned helped you understand God better?

How has what you learned helped you understand yourself better?

Review the memory verse from Lesson 10:

> Your word is a lamp for my feet, a light on my path. —**Psalm 119:105**

DISCUSSING THE INMATE CHALLENGE

What are your initial reactions from the video?

What emotions did you experience while you watched? Why?

*For the eyes of the Lord run to and fro through-
out the whole earth, to give strong support to
those whose heart is blameless toward him.*
—**2 Chronicles 16:9**

George said: "When I read that, I knew at that moment that God wanted to use me. I knew that, in spite of everything that I've done and everything I did up until that moment, God wanted to use me."

Do you feel like God wants to use you?

Describe some of the main challenges you face in terms of being used by God in your current situation.

What are some opportunities for God to use you in your current situation?

Darryl said: "Children are going to emulate us; they're going to pattern their lives after us.... I know some who actually resent their fathers, but they ended up being just like their fathers—the same people they resent. So we have to have that strong relationship with God, because only through that relationship with God are we going to be empowered to be a good example for our children."

Given your current situation, what do you fear most for your children? Why?

What do you want most for your children? Why?

George said: "We must see ourselves as assets.... I don't see myself as a prisoner; I don't see myself as an inmate. I see myself as a son of the living God. I'm blessed. And because my family's connected to me, they're blessed."

*But to all who did receive him, who believed in
his name, he gave the right to become children of
God, who were born, not of blood nor of the will
of the flesh nor of the will of man, but of God.*
—**John 1:12-13**

Do you see yourself the way God sees you? Explain.

What does it mean to be children of God, in your experience?

Ron said: "There's not a person that's in prison that does not deal
with loneliness.... But I believe that God is able, in those moments,
to give us His loving-kindness and to wrap His arms around us."

"The Bible says that in our weaknesses is when His strength is
made perfect. We will never experience God's strength in our lives
until we get to the place where we understand, 'I'm helpless!' "

> *But He said to me, "My grace is sufficient for
> you, for my power is made perfect in weakness."
> Therefore I will boast all the more gladly of my
> weaknesses, so that the power of Christ may
> rest upon me. For the sake of Christ, then, I am
> content with weaknesses, insults, hardships, per-
> secutions, and calamities. For when I am weak,
> then I am strong.* —**2 Corinthians 12:9-10**

Do you find it easy or difficult to admit your weakness? Explain.

**What does it look like to turn to God when we need help? How do
we find Him?**

Ron said: "I hear this a lot in prison: 'I'm going to wait till I get
out to start going to church. I'm going to wait till I get out to start
serving God. I'm going to wait till I get out to do this and that.' And

guess what—it never happens when you get out. Why? Because you get consumed with what's going on in the world."

What decisions do you need to make while you're in prison?

What steps do you need to take while you're in prison?

What steps do you need to take right now

THE MALACHI DADS PLEDGE

As a Malachi Dad, I solemnly pledge to glorify God and build His Kingdom by prioritizing the raising of godly children, first in my family, then in the influencing of other men to do the same in theirs. I firmly believe that my transformed life in Christ—my life of integrity, pursuit of this vision, and the pursuit of godly character—will allow me to impact my children, family, and others towards this end.

I will practice a life of daily discipline and dependence on God through prayer and the study of God's Word for the wisdom in how to nurture my children in the admonition of the Lord. I will pursue this endeavor for a lifetime whether my children are in my home or not.

Finally, I believe that my end goal is not only for my children to walk in the Lord but this God-given vision would impact multiple generations to come, so help me God.

HOMEWORK

Complete the following assignments before the group gathers for Lesson 12.

Take a moment to think deeply about the following questions, and to answer them honestly from your heart.

1. What kind of man do you want to be after you're finished with prison?

2. What kind of husband do you want to be after you're released from prison?

3. What kind of father do you want to be after you're released?

4. What kind of provider do you want to be once you are released?

5. Do you believe you can become the person you want to be? Explain.

6. How can you start becoming that person now? What steps do you need to take?

Review the verses you learned in the previous lessons.

Lesson 1:

In the beginning, God created the heavens and the earth. —**Genesis 1:1**

Lesson 2:

> For all have sinned and fall short of the glory of God. —**Romans 3:23**

Lesson 3:

> For God so loved the world, that he gave his only Son, that whoever believes in him should not perish but have eternal life. —**John 3:16**

Lesson 4:

> And I will give you a new heart, and a new spirit I will put within you. And I will remove the heart of stone from your flesh and give you a heart of flesh. —**Ezekiel 36:26**

Lesson 5:

> Work out your own salvation with fear and trembling, for it is God who works in you, both to will and to work for his good pleasure. —**Philippians 2:12b-13**

Lesson 6:

> Therefore a man shall leave his father and his mother and hold fast to his wife, and they shall become one flesh. —**Genesis 2:24**

Lesson 7:

> Husbands, love your wives, as Christ loved the church and gave himself up for her. —**Ephesians 5:25**

Lesson 8:

> In the fear of the Lord one has strong confidence, and his children will have a refuge. —**Proverbs 14:26**

Lesson 9:

> *Train up a child in the way he should go; even*
> *when he is old he will not depart from it.*
> **—Proverbs 22:6**

Lesson 10:

> *Your word is a lamp for my feet, a light on my*
> *path.* **—Psalm 119:105**

THE MALACHI DADS PLEDGE

As a Malachi Dad, I solemnly pledge to glorify God and build
His Kingdom by prioritizing the raising of godly children,
first in my family, then in the influencing of other men to
do the same in theirs. I firmly believe that my transformed
life in Christ—my life of integrity, pursuit of this vision, and
the pursuit of godly character—will allow me to impact my
children, family, and others towards this end.

I will practice a life of daily discipline and dependence on God
through prayer and the study of God's Word for the wisdom
in how to nurture my children in the admonition of the Lord.
I will pursue this endeavor for a lifetime whether my children
are in my home or not.

Finally, I believe that my end goal is not only for my children
to walk in the Lord but this God-given vision would impact
multiple generations to come, so help me God.

Review this week's memory verse:

> *And He will turn the hearts of fathers to their*
> *children and the hearts of children to their*
> *fathers.* **—Malachi 4:6**

Inmate Challenge

LESSON 12 **MEMORY VERSE**

Keep your heart with all vigilance,
for from it flow the springs of life.

Proverbs 4:23

FACILITATOR NOTES

KEY TOPICS

• *Show the relationship between behavior and the heart—the inner man.*

• *Reinforce the importance of godly counsel, friends and choices.*

• *Demonstrate the consequences of choices.*

LARGE GROUP NOTES

Begin with an opening prayer.

Remind participants of the main purpose of this study: to provide an overview of what the Bible says about God, man, marriage and parenting.

Review the Malachi Dads Pledge.

Use the questions on pages 184–186 to address what God desires for our inner selves.

Be sure to create the case for why following God is a better path to choose for life then following after sinful desires.

Focus your teaching time in the large group on Galatians 6:8. Paul uses the imagery of farming in this verse. The idea of sowing and reaping is seen twice in this verse; both times the idea he is expressing to the Galatians is that the choices you make will directly affect your consequences. We get the idea of "reaping what you sow" from this verse.

SMALL GROUP NOTES

Divide the large group into smaller groups of four to six people (depending on the number of facilitators available). Use the questions on page 186 to review the homework from Lesson 11.

Recite the memory verse from Lesson 11:

> And he will turn the hearts of fathers to their children and the hearts of children to their fathers. **—Malachi 4:6**

Discuss the main topics of this week's lesson using the material on pages 187-191.

Recite this week's memory verse:

> Keep your heart with all vigilance, for from it flow the springs of life. **—Proverbs 4:23**

In the small group time be sure to express that the choices each person makes are a reflection of their heart. One of the major themes of this book is the "two path" concept. Be sure to remind the small group that the heart is the center for each unique person and that the choices that are made spring from who you are. There are consequences on all our choices both for good and bad. How you decide will affect the paths you go down in your life.

Close the small-group discussion with a time of prayer.

Lesson 12

THE HEART

LARGE GROUP SESSION

REVIEW LESSON 11

Recite the Malachi Dads Pledge:

As a Malachi Dad, I solemnly pledge to glorify God and build His Kingdom by prioritizing the raising of godly children, first in my family, then in the influencing of other men to do the same in theirs. I firmly believe that my transformed life in Christ—my life of integrity, pursuit of this vision, and the pursuit of godly character—will allow me to impact my children, family, and others towards this end.

I will practice a life of daily discipline and dependence on God through prayer and the study of God's Word for the wisdom in how to nurture my children in the admonition of the Lord. I will pursue this endeavor for a lifetime whether my children are in my home or not.

Finally, I believe that my end goal is not only for my children to walk in the Lord but this God-given vision would impact multiple generations to come, so help me God.

KEY OBJECTIVES

Here are the key objectives for discussion this week:

- Show the relationship between behavior and the heart—the inner man.

- Reinforce the importance of godly counsel, friends, and choices.

- Demonstrate the consequences of choices. There are two choices to make: You can choose to follow God in obedience, or you can follow after the temptations of this world and your own sinful desires. Each believer will face the consequences for their choices.

THE HEART

Do you think it's easier to live as a Christian or a nonbeliever? Explain.

One of the things the Bible makes clear is that a life spent in rebellion against God is difficult and filled with trouble.

> *There is a way that seems right to a man, but its end is the way to death.* —**Proverbs 16:25**

> *Good sense wins favor, but the way of the treacherous is their ruin.* —**Proverbs 13:15**

> *For the one who sows to his own flesh will from the flesh reap corruption, but the one who sows to the Spirit will from the Spirit reap eternal life.* —**Galatians 6:8**

How have you experienced the difficult consequences of rebelling against God?

Where do you see evidence in our culture that choosing to walk away from God causes many problems?

When we choose to walk in submission to God, our lives become much simpler. This doesn't mean we won't ever have problems or that we'll always get what we want. Rather, it means that we will find peace even in difficult circumstances because we know God is in control.

> Come to me, all who labor and are heavy laden, and I will give you rest. Take my yoke upon you, and learn from me, for I am gentle and lowly in heart, and you will find rest for your souls. For my yoke is easy, and my burden is light. —**Matthew 11:28-30**

When have you felt like you were desperate for rest?

> The thief comes only to steal and kill and destroy. I came that they may have life and have it abundantly. —**John 10:10**

> But the fruit of the Spirit is love, joy, peace, patience, kindness, goodness, faithfulness, gentleness, self-control; against such things there is no law. —**Galatians 5:22-23**

How have you experienced the benefits of following God?

Because of sin, we're not able to follow God and obey His plans for our life under our own power. Instead, God transforms us from the inside out, giving us a new heart—a new inner self.

> And I will give them one heart, and a new spirit I will put within them. I will remove the heart of

stone from their flesh and give them a heart of flesh, that they may walk in my statutes and keep my rules and obey them. And they shall be my people, and I will be their God. —**Ezekiel 11:19-20**

How do we know if God has given us a new heart and empowered us to follow Him? If we begin to demonstrate godly habits in our lives. Here are some practical thoughts on what it means to practice godly habits:

- Our primary goal in life should be to please God (2 Corinthians 5:9). This is the starting point for godly habits.

- We please God by acting more and more like Jesus Christ.
    Matthew 3:17
    Romans 8:28-29

- God knows we will never be perfect, but He wants us to grow through the power of the Holy Spirit.
    Ephesians 4:22-24
    2 Peter 3:18

What habits would you like to develop as you continue living for God?

SMALL GROUP SESSION

REVIEW

What are some words that describe the kind of man you want to become?

How will you take the first step in order to become that person?

Recite the memory verse from Lesson 11:

> *And he will turn the hearts of fathers to their children and the hearts of children to their fathers.* —**Malachi 4:6**

DISCUSSING THE HEART

Following God will lead us to many decision points where we must choose to obey what God wants us to do or take action based on our own desires. The choices we make when confronted with these decision points will reveal the condition of our hearts.

> *For the word of God is living and active, sharper than any two-edged sword, piercing to the division of soul and of spirit, of joints and of marrow, and discerning the thoughts and intentions of the heart. And no creature is hidden from his sight, but all are naked and exposed to the eyes of him to whom we must give account.* —**Hebrews 4:12-13**

What's your initial reaction to these verses? Why?

What can we hide from God?

Remember from lesson 4 in this book the heart describes the character and identity of the person. Your heart is what makes you, you. The choices that are made moment by moment are a reflection of your heart.

There are several attitudes or "heart conditions" that God wants us to avoid if we are to follow Him. First, the Bible teaches us not to have a double-minded heart. This is the kind of heart that knows one thing to be true, but behaves in a way that goes against the truth.

> Draw near to God, and he will draw near to you.
> Cleanse your hands, you sinners, and purify your
> hearts, you double-minded. —**James 4:8**

> Therefore you have no excuse, O man, every one
> of you who judges. For in passing judgment on
> another you condemn yourself, because you, the
> judge, practice the very same things. We know
> that the judgment of God rightly falls on those
> who practice such things. Do you suppose, O
> man—you who judge those who practice such
> things and yet do them yourself—that you will
> escape the judgment of God? —**Romans 2:1-3**

Why is it so easy for us to make choices in life that are hypocritical?

Second, God wants us to avoid hearts that are filled with bitterness. Bitterness is a foothold for resentment and the origin of anger. Therefore, a heart of bitterness not only affects the person who is bitter, but also the people around that person in a very destructive way.

> When my soul was embittered, when I was
> pricked in heart, I was brutish and ignorant; I was
> like a beast toward you. —**Psalm 73:21-22**

> See to it that no one fails to obtain the grace of
> God; that no "root of bitterness" springs up and
> causes trouble, and by it many become defiled.
> —**Hebrews 12:15**

The Heart

What about your current situation makes it easy for bitterness to reside in your heart?

How can you fight against bitterness?

Third, God wants us to avoid pride in our hearts. Pride clouds our thinking and affects our behavior. To avoid pride, however, we must be humble.

> *Pride goes before destruction, and a haughty spirit before a fall.* —**Proverbs 16:18**

> *For the wicked boasts of the desires of his soul, and the one greedy for gain curses and renounces the Lord. In the pride of his face the wicked does not seek him; all his thoughts are, "There is no God."* —**Psalm 10:3-4**

Describe the symptoms of a heart that is struggling with pride.

What are some ways to grow in humility as a follower of God?

So far we've looked at several characteristics and choices that God wants us to avoid. Now let's look at the kind of heart God wants us to develop as His spirit changes us from the inside out.

First, God wants us to develop hearts that are clean. This means we must repent of our sins and ask forgiveness from God. God will do His part to create the clean heart, but we have to be willing to repent (turn away from) the sin that brought about the unclean condition in the first place.

> *Create in me a clean heart, O God, and renew a right spirit within me.* —**Psalm 51:10**

Why is it that God must create a clean heart inside of us, instead of us choosing to clean ourselves?

What emotions do you experience when you think about the opportunity to have a clean heart? Why?

Second, God wants us to develop glad hearts as we live for Him. One part of the fruit of the spirit is joy. Therefore, joy is evidence of the Spirit's work in a person's heart and life. People with a glad heart focus on three things: who God is (Psalm 104); what God has done (Psalm 107); and what God will do (Psalm 110).

> *Therefore my heart is glad, and my whole being rejoices; my flesh also dwells secure.* —**Psalm 16:9**

Finally, God wants us to develop hearts that are steadfast as we follow Him. A steadfast heart doesn't quit; it doesn't give up, and it's not easily moved when the winds of trials and pressures come its way. That's because such hearts are focused on God's steadfast love (Psalm 107:43), faithfulness (Psalm 108:4), and God's deliverance and power (Psalm 108:13).

> *They set a net for my steps; my soul was bowed down. They dug a pit in my way, but they have fallen into it themselves. Selah. My heart is steadfast, O God, my heart is steadfast!*
> —**Psalm 57:6-7a**

> *My heart is steadfast, O God! I will sing and make melody with all my being!* —**Psalm 108:1**

Why is steadfastness an important quality for men who are incarcerated?

What obstacles get in the way of us developing the kinds of characteristics God desires?

How can these obstacles be overcome?

We've spent 12 lessons exploring what it means to be a man of God, including the characteristics of a godly husband and a godly father. Let's remember that in order to become the kind of man we want to be, we must rely on God's power to create a new heart within us.

THE MALACHI DADS PLEDGE

As a Malachi Dad, I solemnly pledge to glorify God and build His Kingdom by prioritizing the raising of godly children, first in my family, then in the influencing of other men to do the same in theirs. I firmly believe that my transformed life in Christ—my life of integrity, pursuit of this vision, and the pursuit of godly character—will allow me to impact my children, family, and others towards this end.

I will practice a life of daily discipline and dependence on God through prayer and the study of God's Word for the wisdom in how to nurture my children in the admonition of the Lord. I will pursue this endeavor for a lifetime whether my children are in my home or not.

Finally, I believe that my end goal is not only for my children to walk in the Lord but this God-given vision would impact multiple generations to come, so help me God.

Name: _____ Date: ___/___/___

CAN YOU TRUST THE BIBLE?

In our Malachi Dads program, we believe that the Bible is the final source of authority in the life of a believer. This is why we heavily incorporate the Scriptures throughout the lessons in the Malachi Dads curriculum. The most important thing for every believer is to hear God's truth from His Word. The Bible is the real curriculum for Malachi Dads. It is the truth of Scripture that the Holy Spirit uses to change our hearts.

So, the question really is: "Can you trust the Bible?" Each time you open up the pages of the Bible can you know with confidence that you are reading the truth that comes from God? We hope this addition to the Malachi Dads book gives you facts and evidence to confirm that the Scriptures you read are reliable and worthy of the time you spend in reading what God has for you.

There are six parts listed below that provide evidence to answer the question: "Can you can trust the Bible?"

1. **The first fact for us to explore is that the Scriptures claim to come from God.** We believe that God is the ultimate source of truth (Exodus 34:6, Psalm 25:5, John 14:6) and if He has given us His Word in the pages of the Bible, then that Word would be true (John 17:17).

   People who are skeptical of the Bible often claim that Christians have made up the divine origins of God's Word. They claim that the Bible says nothing about being inspired by God. This is not true.

The Bible claims in several places to be divinely inspired (written by God through human personalities), including these verses:

> Knowing this first of all, that no prophecy of Scripture comes from someone's own interpretation. For no prophecy was ever produced by the will of man, but men spoke from God as they were carried along by the Holy Spirit. —**2 Peter 1:20-21**

> All Scripture is breathed out by God and profitable for teaching, for reproof, for correction, and for training in righteousness. —**2 Timothy 3:16**

The Old Testament Scriptures also make the claim to be God's Words (Psalm 19:7-11; Jeremiah 36:1-4; Ezekiel 2:4).

CONCLUSION: The Bible claims to be a supernatural collection of books that are divinely inspired by God.

2. **The second point we want to make is that the Bible is a very unique book, like no other book ever written.** Listed below are some of those unique facts about the Bible:

The Bible was written by approximately 40 men. These men were from all walks of life: kings, peasants, fishermen, physicians, statesmen, scholars, poets, and farmers. Each of these men was inspired by God through the Holy Spirit, but they wrote one or more books of the Bible in their own style and personality.

The first parts of the Bible were written before 1,500 B.C., and the last books were written around A.D. 100. That means the Bible was written over a period of more than 1,600 years.

Even though the Bible was written by about 40 men who lived during this 1,600-year time period, the text of God's Word is consistent throughout. Everything fits together and communicates the same message about God, people, sin, and salvation.

The Bible was written using three different languages: The majority of the Old Testament is written in the Hebrew language, with a couple sections in the Old Testament written in Aramaic. The New Testament is written in the common Greek language that was used during that period of time.

The Bible remained consistent because it ultimately came from God.

CONCLUSION: The Bible is trustworthy and reliable.

3. **The third fact that should give you confidence when you read the Bible is that the Scriptures are reliable and have not changed over time.**

Time is one of the factors scholars use to decide whether an ancient book is reliable. Specifically, they look at the amount of time between the date a book was first written and the date of the oldest copy found. For example, if a book was written in A.D. 500 and the oldest copy available today was made in A.D. 1500, the difference would be 1,000 years from the time that the original was written until the earliest copy of that book was found.

Here are some of the amounts of years of difference between the original writing and the oldest available copies found from a few famous authors that people consider reliable:

- *Aristotle:* 1,400 years from the original writing to the earliest found copy
- *Caesar:* 1,000 years from the original writing to the earliest found copy
- *Plato:* 1,200 years from the original writing to the earliest found copy

The amount of time between when the original books of the New Testament were written and the earliest copies that have been discovered to date is less than 100 years.

Not only are the manuscripts of the Scriptures that have been found by scholars much closer to the originals, but the amount of manuscripts found is greater than any other ancient book:

- *Aristotle* – 49 copies
- *Caesar* – 10 copies
- *Plato* – 7 copies
- *Homer's Iliad* – around 2,000
- *New Testament* – 5,600 Greek copies. When you count the early Latin and other sources that quote a passage of the Scriptures there are about 24,000 copies or portions of the New Testament found.

CONCLUSION: The Bible is the most reliable ancient book ever written, and we can be confident that we have an accurate witness to the original writings.

4. One of the special features of the Bible are the numerous prophetic statements that are found in the Scriptures.

There are places in the Bible where God told people what would happen in the future—this is called prophecy. Many of God's prophecies have already taken place, but some are still in the future.

Here are some of the biblical prophecies that have already been fulfilled:

- God spoke through the prophet Jeremiah to prophesy that the people of Jerusalem would be captives in Babylon for 70 years (see Jeremiah 25:11-12). The first set of captivity to Babylon happened in 606 B.C., and the first group of returning Jews of Jerusalem took place in 536 B.C., under Zerubbabel.

- God spoke through the prophet Amos to prophesy about 760 B.C. that the nation of Israel would be reestablished after being destroyed (Amos 9:14-15). It happened in 1948.

- Several aspects of Jesus' life were prophesied in the Old Testament, including His birth in Bethlehem, His mother being a virgin, His betrayal for 30 pieces of silver, His death, His resurrection and many more.

- Jesus also made prophetic statements during his ministry. When his disciples made some statements to him concerning the beauty of the Temple in Jerusalem, he stated that the Temple (Matthew 24:1-2) would be destroyed. This was fulfilled in AD 70 about 37 years later when the Roman general Titus destroyed the Temple and much of the city of Jerusalem.

CONCLUSION: The prophecies that have come true are one of the reasons we can trust the Bible as a supernatural book—something that comes from God.

5. **Another evidence to the reliability of Scripture can be found not from within its pages, but from historical records.** Science has proven the Bible to be reliable through its discoveries.

- The Bible describes many cities, kingdoms and kings that were lost over the centuries—archeologists used to have no record of them outside of God's Word. As a result, many believed that the people and events described in the Bible were myths. However, with the advancement of archeology, scholars have found the Bible to be a reliable tool in their research.

- Around 1800, several European nations (France and England especially) began excavating sites of ancient civilizations in the Middle East, which is how the science of archaeology began.

- Over the past 200 years, archaeologists have found the

location of many biblical cities and discovered the timelines of their kings. Scientists have also provided a glimpse into the daily life of people during Old Testament times as numerous ancient languages have been decoded and thousands of texts translated.

- Archaeology now relies heavily on the biblical text for clues to the location of ancient cities, the dates of kings and kingdoms, and the location and dates of significant battles.

CONCLUSION: The science of archaeology confirms rather than disproves the statements of the Bible.

6. **The impact that the Bible has made on our culture cannot be ignored.** No other book has helped to shape and mold our history and modern life. From the phrases and words we use to this day, the traditions of worship that are available, and the form of government that we have; all these can be traced back to the Bible.

In recent centuries, the English language has adopted many expressions based on the Bible. These expressions entered the language during a time when more people read the Bible and were familiar with what it said. Here are some of the expressions or phrases found in the Bible that we still use today:

- *An eye for an eye* (Leviticus 24:19-20)
- *By the skin of my teeth* (Job 19:20)
- *Dust to dust* (Genesis 3:19)
- *A drop in the bucket* (Isaiah 40:15)
- *Sour grapes* (Ezekiel 18:2)
- *To cast the first stone* (John 8:7)

It is because of the truth found in the Bible that there have been those throughout history that made significant changes that had a major impact on history. One of these people that was used by God to make a significant change in the history of the church was Martin Luther. Reading the truth of the Bible motivated him to make some needed changes in the church.

- The Bible has been the foundation for many cultural changes throughout the centuries, including the Protestant Reformation.

- For many years, there was only one kind of Christian church in the world. This was a good thing and helped the church spread a unified message. Slowly, however, the early church began to drift away from biblical teaching, and the people in charge began to seek out corrupt practices and teach false doctrine.

- In 1517, a man named Martin Luther posted 95 discussion points on his local church door. These were 95 ways he felt the church was working against the Bible. This was the beginning of what we now call the Protestant Reformation. As a result of Luther's dedication to God's Word, the Protestant church was born. Churches around the world recommitted to teaching the truths of God's Word—that salvation is by faith alone, in Christ alone, on the authority of the Bible alone, and all to the glory of God.

The founding fathers of the United States used many principles they found within the pages of the Bible to write its founding documents:

- The U.S. Constitution is based on a biblical view of man, government, and justice. The writers understood the sinfulness of man as taught from the Scriptures and did their part to write in limits to check any one person from gaining too much power.

- The writers of the Declaration of Independence also believed in the creation of human beings in the image of God and that each individual was endowed with certain inalienable rights. Every human being has worth and dignity.

- The foundation of the United States is based on Christian values, and those values were found by the writers of the Constitution within the pages of Scripture.

There are books written about everything, but there is only one book written that helps to answer the most important questions that humans ask.

- We could fill entire libraries with all the books that have been published in order to answer the bigger questions about life and happiness. But that would be wasteful and unnecessary.

- That's because the Bible answers all of man's greatest questions, including:

  Where did I come from?

  What is my purpose?

- The Bible covers all areas of life, including:

  Family and parenting

  Anthropology, sociology, psychology

  Government, labor, the church, science, language, and history.

CONCLUSION: The Bible is an important source for today's culture.

Hopefully you have found this section helpful in gaining a greater trust in the Scriptures. God has given His children His Word so that we can live for Him. It is His Word, the Bible, that is our final source of truth. It is a gift from Him that He has given so that believers can know Him, and what He desires from his children.

> *So shall my word be that goes out from my mouth; it shall not return to me empty, but it shall accomplish that which I purpose, and shall succeed in the thing for which I sent it.* **—Isaiah 55:11**

SUGGESTED 30 DAY BIBLE READING PLAN

Here is a suggested plan to help get you into the habit of reading God's Word each day. There are many great plans and strategies for reading through the Bible. This plan will highlight several major sections from the whole Bible so that you can get a good overview of God's Word. Remember this plan just highlights several parts of the Bible:

Day 1	Genesis 1-2	Day 16	John 11
Day 2	Genesis 3	Day 17	John 17
Day 3	Genesis 15-17	Day 18	Matthew 26-27
Day 4	Exodus 3-4	Day 19	John 20
Day 5	Exodus 20	Day 20	Luke 24
Day 6	1 Samuel 16-17	Day 21	Acts 2
Day 7	1 Kings 18	Day 22	Acts 9
Day 8	Daniel 2-3	Day 23	Acts 26
Day 9	Isaiah 9, 53, 61	Day 24	Romans 3
Day 10	Luke 1-2	Day 25	Romans 7-8
Day 11	John 1	Day 26	1 Corinthians 13
Day 12	Luke 4	Day 27	Ephesians 6
Day 13	Matthew 5-8	Day 28	Colossians 3
Day 14	John 3	Day 29	James 1
Day 15	John 5	Day 30	Revelation 21-22

NOTES

NOTES

NOTES

NOTES

MORE FROM LIFELINE GLOBAL MINISTRIES™

Malachi Dads™ and Hannah's Gift™ programs are in prisons and jails throughout the United States and internationally. Lifeline Global Ministries™ helps to restore and equip incarcerated men and women to become godly parents so that the generational cycle of incarceration can be broken. ***To find out how you can order Lifeline Global Ministries™ curriculum, please visit the website at www.lifelineglobal.org.***

Malachi Dads™ — Psalm 1 – The Blessed Man

Reflect on Psalm 1 in this six-week study written by inmates from the Malachi Dads™ program who have been transformed by the gospel of Jesus Christ. You'll study the characteristics of a godly man found in the six verses of Psalm 1. Chapters include explanations of each verse, review questions and homework to help readers live out the lesson. Men from the Malachi Dads™ program also share their personal testimonies througout the book. ***Also available in Spanish.***

Malachi Dads™ — The Heart of a Man – Part 1

This 12-lesson study teaches incarcerated fathers how they can have a heart that pleases God, regardless of their past sins. Helps fathers in prison understand what it means to be men after God's own heart. This Malachi Dads™ study has memory verses and assignments. Topics cover trust-worthiness, temptations and purity, prayer, and more. ***Also available in Spanish.***

Malachi Dads™ — The Heart of a Man Part 2

Continue *The Heart of a Man* study with new lessons that address how to develop godly character and integrity in your walk with God. Includes lessons designed to help men live as godly examples in their families and communities. This curriculum for men's prison ministry provides practical, biblical advice for life, marriage and parenting. ***Also available in Spanish.***

Malachi Dads™ — The Heart of a Father Six-Week Study

This six-week study for men's prison ministry provides practical biblical advice for life, marriage, and parenting. Quickly growing as a significant force in fathering, the Malachi Dads program is designed for fathers in the most broken of places—prison. It shows men how to become Christ-followers and grow in their faith.

Malachi Dads™ — Family Restoration
Powerful lessons based on the book of Jeremiah that teach incarcerated fathers about healthy communication, authority, the promise of restoration, and more.

Malachi Dads™ — Inmate Challenge DVD
This DVD component of the Malachi Dads™ The Heart of a Father curriculum was filmed on location at the famed Angola Prison in Louisiana. Three inmate fathers share their stories and their challenge to other inmates. This DVD is an ideal launching point for jail or prison ministry and for challenging fathers to consider the legacy they are leaving. Includes a five-week small group discussion guide. *To order your copy of the Inmate Challenge DVD, visit the Lifeline Global Ministries™ website: www.lifelinegobal.org, or your Lifeline mentor.*

Hannah's Gift™ — Psalm 23
This powerful six-lesson devotional helps you reflect on the many ways God is always with us as our Shepherd, our Peace, our Provider, our Victory, our Righteousness and our Healer. Written by inmates at Louisiana Correctional Institution for Women who are taking part in the Hannah's Gift™ prison ministry, each lesson includes a personal testimony and brief devotional, discussion questions, and verses to memorize.

Hannah's Gift™ — The Heart of a Mother
Hannah's Gift™ is a 12-week program especially for women's prison ministry. *The Heart of a Mother* is modeled after the life of Hannah and her son as told in the first two chapters of 1 Samuel in the Old Testament. This curriculum offers mothers the opportunity to parent from a distance and give a legacy of faith to their children. **Also available in Spanish.**

Hannah's Gift™ — Family Restoration
This study provides incarcerated mothers biblical steps for building healthy family relationships straight from God's Word. This powerful, easy-to-follow devotional has 10 lessons from the book of Jeremiah. Each lesson includes a memory verse and five days' worth of study materials, devotionals, and assignments. Topics include healthy communication, authority, and the promise of restoration.

Hannah's Gift™ — Beautiful Woman

This book identifies key struggles that trip women up and cause them to forfeit their happiness and joy. It helps women to see that the rules they have been playing by will lead to defeat. It shows them a better way out of their chaos through the truth of God's Word. These 10 lessons are designed to help women find their place as Beautiful Women in this world.

Equip Leaders

This easy-to-follow guide trains Malachi Dads™ and Hannah's Gift™ facilitators to effecitvely lead inmate small groups. Each chapter gives readers key verses, biblical foundations, methods, teaching pointers, and more for leading small groups. Topics include ministry for life change, hand on the Word, and gospel of grace.

ORDER TODAY!

To find out how you can order Lifeline Global Ministries™ curriculum, please visit the website at **www.lifelineglobal.org.**